GOOD CHOICES

How to Become Spiritually Mature by Making Right Decisions

KEITH GENTRY

malcolm down

PUBLISHING

Acknowledgements

Thanks to my supportive family, the three Js: Janice, who made me keep re-writing the book until it made sense; and my children Joshua and Jazmin.

To you, the reader, this book is written for your better understanding of being able to be a blessing to others.

Additionally, many thanks to friends who supported and helped with proof reading and getting this book launched.

Moreover, brothers, we want you to experience the grace of God bestowed on the churches of Macedonia, how in a great trial of affliction, the abundance of their joy and their deep poverty overflowed toward the riches of their generous giving. For I bear record that according to their means, and beyond their means, they freely gave, begging us with much urgency that we would receive the gift and the fellowship of ministering to the saints. This they did, not as we expected. First, they gave themselves to the Lord, and then to us by the will of God. So we urged Titus, that as he had begun, so he would also complete this gracious deed for you. But as you abound in everything – in faith, in utterance, in knowledge, in all diligence, and in your love to us – see that you abound in this grace also.

2 Corinthians 8:1–7

Foreword by Rev Aubrey Longmore

Keith is a committed Christian. I have known him for more than twenty five years. His wife Janice, son Joshua and daughter Jasmin are all outstanding members of the Milton Keynes community. Keith is a preacher of the gospel of Jesus Christ and regularly preaches in his local church as well as in many other parts of the United Kingdom. Keith has been an inspiration to me and to many in his pursuit of excellence in all of his endeavours.

Keith's latest book, *Good Choices*, highlights one of the high roads to spiritual maturity and success. In *Good Choices* there is a rare focus on the unexcelled kindness of the Macedonian churches towards those experiencing difficulties of various kinds. Readers will get a revelatory insight into Holy Ghost-inspired kindness, possibly unparalleled in the Holy Scriptures. We will see that the Macedonians' exceptional generosity was matched only by the poor widow who, while being unknowingly observed by the Lord, gave her all – the kingly sum of two mites.

By the Macedonian model, Keith shows that they themselves were in poverty, dealing with their own trial of affliction. They were hungry and experiencing great lack. Yet, in spite of their own adverse situation, they willingly gave to the ministry so much so that they were able to support Titus and send him to save the wealthiest region of churches in Corinth. In addition, they did it all with 'joy', and 'beyond their means'.

In his book, Keith shares keys to unlock clues within the Word of God to enable the reader to be more discerning and productive with the investment of their time, effort and money in the spiritual and natural choices of life. Assured of the infallibility of the Word of God, Keith is convinced that if the reader is willing to invest time in spiritual disciplines, as well as in listening to God's inward voice, reading and meditating on the Word for guidance, then ultimate success is assured.

As Keith develops his thoughts on the Macedonian churches, he shows that they were amongst the poorest of the poor. We'll see that Titus, a young preacher, was funded by the Macedonian churches to go on a missionary trip to the Corinthians. The Macedonians sacrifice is heightened when we realise that the Corinthians to whom Titus was going were amongst the wealthiest of the churches. Normal human reasoning would beg the question, 'Why wouldn't the Corinthians fund their own needs by sending Titus the necessary funds required for this endeavour?'

The many principles outlined in *Good Choices* should help any Christian attain spiritual maturity. Not confined to Christendom though, much help is also offered to business people, charitable givers and young families staring out in life, as well as to the more settled 50's and 60's.

Although this is a book that focuses on the unmatched giving of 'a group of poor needy churches', the secret of giving is also shown by several wealthy people who have discovered and practise the principle of giving. Successful wealthy givers shown include John Timpson, Richard Branson, Bill Gates, Oprah Winfrey, Steven Spielberg and the late Diana Princess of Wales.

In contrast to the millionaires and billionaires who give of their vast wealth are the Macedonians churches that gave out of their meagre means. This group of churches in Macedonia constituted the poorest group of churches anywhere in the inspired Word of God. They remain the yardstick of unsurpassed kindness and generosity anywhere in the Word of God and today still serve as a yardstick of success for our generation.

Contents

Preface

◌◠◌

Prior to the financial crash of 2008, in many churches and in many countries around the world, there had been an influence of prosperity leading to the spirit of greed, which wormed its way across the world. Within many churches I noticed that scriptures and stories from the Bible had been stretched and distorted by this spirit of greed, rather than there being a focus on making good choices in life.

This book is aimed at helping people understand the Bible better about making good choices, whatever the circumstances. It details some of the spiritual and natural truths about making good choices in your spiritual life, family, home and church for economic well-being.

While I was writing this book, I found that I started to form different habits, which I wish to share with the reader to encourage them. I hope they rub off on you. This book is about making the right decisions when we are confronted with choices in life, allowing time to evaluate the risks without delaying the journey of an expected outcome. As I move through the book I will affirm this book is about making good choices. From time to time I will talk about investments. I use the word 'investments' concurrently, as I would use the word 'choices'. I am hoping and wishing to enable the reader and encourage them to make good choices. This book is not about how to become greedy, but rather to avoid lack or disappointment. If we can avoid lack, then we would have done well. Never wish to be rich nor poor. King Solomon wrote, *'Do not labour to be rich; cease from your own wisdom.'*[1] Note in verse five, the riches fly away. Additionally, Solomon went on to say, *'Give me neither poverty nor riches.'*[2] These scriptures are comforting and suggest that God will look after our needs, not our greed.

When people stay in debt or remain in a poor state, it is very hard for them to reach their full potential. That does not mean that they will not be able to do something extraordinary. Neither the contents of this book nor I will write anybody off; far from it. As we look at the group of churches in the Macedonian region, they started off in their own will, and God blessed them. They went the extra mile; so much so, it was recorded; they went beyond their own power.

In the world today people observe and understand the natural seasons of when best to till the ground, when to sow, water and reap the harvest. Understanding the background of the natural will enable our spiritual understanding to observe the spiritual process of sowing (investing, time, effort and money) and reaping (helping others, rewards and profits). The difference with the understanding and spiritual intelligence of being a Christian is that we know we can sow even in famine and still receive our harvest.

Just like Isaac sowed in famine and received a hundred fold, so the churches in the poorest parts of Greece, the churches in the Macedonia region, sowed to save the richest church failing in Corinth and falling into deeper sin as outlined in 2 Corinthians 8:1–7 (this is what inspired me to write this book).

The key to *Good Choices* is that the poorest people in the Macedonian churches sowed in faith, with great generosity, and trusted God to help a very prosperous Corinthian church heading for spiritual disaster. This story inspired me because the Macedonian churches saw the need to help someone when they themselves were in greater need. This is the complete opposite of what one would expect. It was literally beyond their means. This is what gripped me to study this passage of Scripture further.

In contrast, to wait for our 'windfall' or spoils in order to help others is not demonstrating total faith beyond what we can see. Abraham gave a tenth from his spoils, introducing the concept and the process of tithing to fund a church that is not supported by any other means, whereas the Macedonian churches gave from their hearts when they had very little – just like the widow's mite. They gave more than a tenth out of their reserves, with no expectation of receiving anything back from their gift of love.

With this contextual focus on the Macedonian church members within this book, one of my objectives is to remind us that 'God's ways are not our ways'. Sometimes we may not understand the circumstances that we find ourselves in and how God works, and therefore I have provided a whole chapter on this thought. God works completely differently to our normal way of thinking.

'For My thoughts are not your thoughts, nor are your ways My ways, says the Lord.'[3]

When the Macedonians were living in poverty, they made a great choice to invest into another prosperous group of people and gave.

My aspirations for this book are:

- To unlock some clues within the Word of God to enable the reader to be more discerning and productive when they invest their time, effort and money in the spiritual and natural choices of life. Good choices come about by implementing knowledge, understanding and wisdom along with spiritual mapping skills using the Word of God and what Jesus taught in his parables. If the reader is willing to invest some time in homework with the added bonus of listening to God's voice and reading his Word for guidance, then a balance can be found to avoid looking only at the prosperity scriptures.
- The reader will definitely think of helping others regardless of their current situation and actively make a difference in their local church and community.
- The reader will experience a better relationship with God and his people following the implementation of God's principles in making good decisions. The reader will be able to experience the grace of God as the churches in Macedonia experienced the Holy Spirit at work in the first century.
- You will be able to use your faith to step forward and be more productive and make a difference in your life and the lives of others.

Endnotes
1. Proverbs 23:4
2. Proverbs 30:8
3. Isaiah 55:8

1
Good Choices: A Holistic View
∽

Read 2 Corinthians 8:1–7

Have you ever observed the seasons and how they are always changing? Notice how they blend into one another over a twelve-month cycle. These four changing seasons are seen by man and often described as 'nature' or how 'Mother Earth' works. When people talk about 'nature' or 'Mother Earth' they are actually talking about a God-given principle of four seasons, and it was God who planned the weather and the seasons; it was God who created heaven and earth. *'While the earth remains, seedtime and harvest, cold and heat, summer and winter, and day and night will not cease.'*[1]

The number four in the Bible means creative, so in every annual cycle something is created. That is why every year is different to the next. In every cycle there is a season to sow and a season to harvest. God has designed times and seasons to allow our decision making to take effect, albeit in the natural or the spiritual. God has given us seedtime and harvest. As long as the farmer prepares the soil and sows the seeds, there is potential for the farmer to look forward to a great harvest and God will bless the seeds sown with the rain and sunshine.

Good choices and speculations only come about by sowing

into something that, in most cases, cannot be seen. The most important things in life cannot be seen. Air, for instance cannot be seen, but we cannot live without it. Let's look at the arable farmer. Arable farming is closer to the natural and spiritual comparison, relating to sowing and reaping and learning to weather the storm naturally and spiritually. On the spiritual side, to gain the spiritual harvest of a soul won for Christ, it takes hours of prayer and patience with and for that person to be born again and be fully involved with a purpose in the Kingdom of God. The farmer knows the risks that may occur within the next year: floods, early frosts and disease are just a few things that can put a farmer off from sowing. However, the arable farmer in faith will sow his seeds in the prepared soil with expectation. Each year, the arable farmer, for example, sows to serve the community which needs to purchase the outcomes of the seed (the spoils of the farmer's labour and faith). The patience of the farmer needs to be steadfast, as ploughing, tilling the soil, sowing, germinating and waiting for the crops to grow all take time before the farmer can experience the full-blown harvest. The original arable process should not be rushed to get the flavour of the harvest just right.

The original seed, which is dead, comes alive again following the planting and watering of the seed (the germination process).

The key to understanding seedtime is to not believe in fairy tales. Jack and the Beanstalk is a great fairy tale. It is about some magic beans that were thrown out of a window and produced an overnight success. When Jack got up in the morning his beans had reached outstanding new heights. In the world today, there will always be websites and books about how to get rich quick, because on the whole many people want to hear how to make money quickly or how to be an overnight success. Maybe Jack's fairy tale has influenced us from a very young age. I am not wishing to write about fairy tales or getting rich quick, but rather about understanding God's processes and how he wishes to bless us according to his plans for us, and our thoughts, abilities and innovations within the natural and spiritual.

Seedtime

Consider the seed for a moment. The seed comes from within the plant, grass, fruit or vegetable. The seeds will be dry and dead.[2] The herb yields seed and the tree yields fruit. The seed is within itself; all planted seed has to be dead. In the natural all animal and human seed has to be kept alive. The seed is sown into soil, it receives moisture and warmth and the seed begins to grow in darkness. The roots appear first and then the seed grows upwards towards the sunlight. Even though the seed cannot see nor can it hear, the seed grows towards the surface. The farmer sometimes suffers famine and floods, yet the seed will still grow. Man will call this seedtime an act of nature; in reality this is an act of God. As God said, *'Let the earth bring forth.'*[3] The seed grows by the faith of God (some may say it is the power or authority of God) as he spoke the original words *'Let there be'*[4] in Genesis. We still need to have faith, too, for things to be planted, sown or built. The same principle of seedtime in the natural is applicable in the natural and spiritual for making good choices, as a seed will grow into something much bigger than the original dead state of the seed. Therefore, if we do not plant the seed, we cannot expect the tree to grow.

In Genesis 26 Isaac sowed at a time of great famine. In fact it was two famines following each other, similar to a double-dip recession[5] that happened in the UK and many parts of the world in 2008 and 2012. The Bible tells us that he received a hundred-fold return. It takes faith in God and understanding of how the seedtime process works, to sow in a double-dip recession.

Since the soil is bone dry, it takes God's providence for the seed to grow. Make no mistake that reaping a harvest in a time of drought, when the ground had been barren for a number of years, was a miracle. What we need to understand is that while he and his family and neighbours were hungry, Isaac needed to wait with patience and long-suffering to receive his full harvest. I believe the people around Isaac would have wanted him to start the harvest early but, like all good things, he needed to wait for the appointed time, even when he could see the seed growing.

To help our comprehension further, let's remember that the cycle of seedtime germination is diverse for every aspect of life, and it is key when trying to understand how long things take to germinate and produce something that meets your expectation.

- When you sow carrot seeds you have to wait about 65 days before they are fully grown to receive an edible crop.
- It takes about two months between sowing sweet potatoes and eating the produce.
- From an acorn we get great oak trees that can live in excess of 400 years, and grow to over 100 feet tall. The oak tree has to wait until it's 20–50 years old before it can produce acorns itself and start the cycle of life again.
- Then there is nine months for a human to be born, whereas elephants have to wait 22 months.

Therefore, every seed has a different 'seedtime purpose' and season. *'To everything there is a season, a time for every purpose under heaven.'*[6]

God is letting us know that there is more than meets our natural eye when we are faced with making a choice; we have a spiritual and natural purpose on earth. What we need to identify is what God has intended for us, and we need to find out what and how our gifts and talents might be used to help others around us.

There are many characters in the Bible we could study to observe what they went through, like Joseph, Abraham, Esther and David. They all started life as a small character to become a main character within the Bible; from a seed to a strong tree producing fruit. Let's look at Joseph.

Joseph's story started with the love of the father, a God-given dream (not a self-manufactured dream) and the jealousy of his brothers.[7] Joseph's dominion over his brothers would take him on many paths from being left to die in a pit, to being sold into slavery, finding favour in Potiphar's house, then false accusations leading to prison.[8]

Yet, there is comfort when things do not go according to our plans, which perhaps we do need to remember. Bad things can happen to anybody. There may be times of sickness, or debt. As the writer to the Hebrews wrote to remind us: *'I will never leave you, nor forsake you.'*[9]

Jesus is always with us, even in the thick of it.

Joseph continued to prosper in prison.[10] Joseph later interpreted the butler's and baker's dreams[11] and eventually, after being forgotten and going through rejection, Joseph was remembered by the butler and called by Pharaoh to interpret his dream and was promoted by Pharaoh for interpreting the dream correctly.[12] Joseph, in exile, found himself second in command of a foreign country. He headed up the country's government, with seven prosperous years followed by seven years of famine, to run the administration and direction of the whole of Egypt.

Between Genesis 37:2 – 41:46 there is a time of unforeseen major disruption of pain, suffering, delay and anguish; a time of tribulation. There were about thirteen years between Joseph being sold into slavery in Egypt to him standing in front of Pharaoh and his dream starting to take shape. Psalms 105:17–22 examines what Joseph went through. In each seed, dream or action plan we plant, we need to understand that there might be times of tribulation. Romans 5:3 suggests that we should glory in tribulation, and have patience. I can relate to Romans 5 as tribulations may be part of life's journey when sowing faith and following God's dream for us. When making choices for the future we may find ourselves in deep water before we reach dry land.

The acorn has to wait over twenty years for it to mature to be able produce other acorns. So when we sow we have to be prepared to wait for the expected outcome. Your faith will always be tested when you sow. When we read about Abraham and Sarah, they had a promise from God that took over twenty-five years for them to experience. In fact, Sarah laughed at the thought that at the age of ninety-nine she would be pregnant. Sarah's personal history was twenty-five years of trying for a child, whilst others around her, such as Hagar the bondwoman, found it easy to give birth. Hagar and her son Ishmael were still in Sarah's household, mocking her for sixteen years or so, behind her back and sometimes openly. Sarah's name means 'the mother of many nations', yet there was no baby in sight. Sarah knew her barren womb was dead. So when she thought of her husband, who was himself one hundred years old, pregnancy would have been a very distant thought. Yet God made it possible by renewing their physical ability. When we sow, God does have a say in what type of return we will reap: *'Be not deceived. God is not mocked. For whatever a man sows, that will he also reap.'*[13]

It was down to their faith in God's Word; when God spoke to them in their old age, that made it possible. The barren womb can produce fruit, even if it looks impossible in the natural. Sarah and Abraham simply needed to believe that it would happen. (It was accounted unto him for righteousness.)

These great stories of faith are in the Bible for our benefit as examples not to give up on God but to believe in him. Jesus said, *'Do not fear. Only believe,'*[14] when healing Jairus' daughter.

For those that are hoping and waiting for the ridiculous blessings promised to us, we must believe, hope for, and have unchanging faith, to move the things that are impossible for us, to the possible with God. *'But Jesus looked at them and said, "With men this is impossible, but with God all things are possible."'*[15]

What happens in nature in the habitat

The environment affects everyone, yet not everyone is concerned about the deteriorating rainforests in the Amazon. If we continue to destroy the forests in Brazil, for example, we run the risk of suffocating ourselves. Rainforests help to provide the clean air we breathe.

My assumption is that every geography teacher around the world teaches the same truth of how trees benefit the air quality and capture the carbon dioxide and turn it into clean oxygen, through the process of photosynthesis. Quite simply, if man keeps cutting down the forests then the earth will be affected. The psalmist wrote '*The earth belongs to the* LORD, *and its fullness, the world, and those who dwell in it*.'[16] The earth is not man's to destroy, so man needs to look after the gift of creation. In Genesis Adam was told to look after the Garden of Eden. Adam was told to '*till it and keep it*'.[17] Why did Adam need to keep a garden that had no thorns or weeds? From the Bible we know that Satan turned up to destroy that wonderful atmosphere and union with God in the Garden of Eden. Adam simply needed to look after the gift that he had been given. Therefore, today we still need to look after and continue to work what has been given to us by God both spiritually or naturally.

Good investments within the family

My immediate family is a family of four, and it is a very busy household. We are probably not dissimilar to many families with a wealth of after-school activities: ballet, rugby, youth clubs, paper rounds, etc.

This list does not even include my own interests or my wife's. When the children were younger we introduced family time on a Monday evening, just to keep the balance. It was a valuable time where we encouraged the children to share their views on their faith, the Word of God, current affairs, school and anything they felt open to discuss. This provided us with an invaluable opportunity to keep abreast of our children's development in a relaxed setting. Children must be encouraged, praised and given direction as there are too many distractions to teach them otherwise. We have had some great sessions over the years, with raised voices, differing opinions, and uncontrollable laughter. Allow your children to express their thoughts, so you know what is within their hearts, so you can support and pray for your children wherever they need direction or help.

In the book of Acts we can experience and feel the paternalistic style of Paul pouring everything he knew from his life's experiences in the natural and spiritual journey as he spoke to Timothy as a father would to his own children.[18] Timothy's father was Greek, his mother was a Jew, and Paul helped Timothy understand the Bible better. Paul saw for himself how rewarding and productive it was to see Timothy mature from Paul's instruction. This is clearly evident when you read the epistles of Timothy. At the beginning, Paul is providing correction and guidance; in the end Timothy is transformed into this strong leader where he is able to lead himself and other churches in the right direction.

Making time for the family is one of the most important, if not *the* most important forms of sowing and certainly an enabler to have a functional and successful family. When we introduced family time, we all had busy lives, or we needed to have a rest following a busy weekend at church and living life after the weekend. However, we made the Monday night our family time moment. Not everyone was comfortable with sharing their thoughts and we tweaked the format to make it more child-friendly and put some fun ice-breakers into the format. Over time the children did open up, and sometimes they even had their own Bible verses for us to discuss. As parents we just provide guidance to keep our children on track in a Christ-like lifestyle.

Sometimes the good seeds that we plant within our children are rejected at the beginning, but after a time of life's experiences, they can then understand why we invested the time at the beginning.

Making good choices for your own health

Our health will benefit from us taking care of it. Just keep living and, without a doubt, we will all find ourselves getting older, and our needs will change depending on what our family or we need. We are all living longer, and sometimes this means that some of us will experience issues with our health. Solomon said, *'But for him who is joined to all the living there is hope, for a living dog is better than a dead lion.'*[19] In other words, it is better to be alive, rather than be a dead king of the animal kingdom because when you are dead, you cannot be of any use. Sometimes people want everything to be in perfect condition before they start something. However, even Paul continued to carry on ministering while it was recorded that he had a thorn in his side relating to some type of pain or illness in his life.

You might not be feeling like a lion but 'just do it'; just get on with your project or activity that God has directed you to do. Caleb is a prime example of an individual who probably did not feel like a lion at the age of eighty-five but decided to take hold of his inheritance. He did not let his age or his physical state interfere with the promise that he knew was his, but in faith he said, *'So now, give me this hill country that the LORD spoke about.'*[20] Caleb fully possessed that mountain and the land had rest from war.

Personally, I have been around the whole spectrum of health for the past fifteen years, from wellness to the pharmaceutical sector. I have noticed that wherever prosperity has been in the past twenty years or so, then the twenty-first-century prosperity diseases such as obesity seem to follow. More than one-third (34.9 per cent or 78.6 million) of US adults are obese.[21] Obesity-related conditions include heart disease, stroke, type 2 diabetes and certain types of cancer; some of the leading causes of preventable death. The estimated annual medical cost of obesity in the US was $147 billion US dollars in 2008; the medical cost for people who were obese was $1,429 higher than those of normal weight. Perhaps too much refined sugar, bleached wheat, salt and less natural organic goodness are some of the main contributors causing these prosperity diseases. In years gone by the well-known global killers such as cancer, heart disease, HIV/AIDS were at the top of news agenda for bad news stories. According to the World Health Organization's fact sheet, of the top ten causes of death (shown on next page), diabetes is now steadily increasing across the world. Diabetes is called the silent killer[22] because it can be in your body for decades before being identified. Currently there is no known cure for this killer disease.

World Health Organization: Fact sheet No 3, 10 May 2011

Top 10 causes of death for the world

Cause	Death in millions	% of deaths
Ischaemic heart disease	7.25	12.8
Stroke and other cerebrovascular disease	6.15	10.8
Lower respiratory infections	3.46	6.1
Chronic obstructive pulmonary disease	3.28	5.8
Diarrhoeal diseases	2.46	4.3
HIV/AIDS	1.78	3.1
Trachea, bronchus, lung cancers	1.39	2.4
Tuberculosis	1.34	2.4
Diabetes mellitus	1.26	2.2
Road traffic accidents	1.21	2.1

The best way to avoid diabetes and similar prosperity diseases as is frequently reported through the media is to make good choices in eating healthily, taking frequent exercise and avoiding too much sugar and salt. It takes real effort to carry it through. The best choice for yourself is to look after your body. You only have one body (temple) so you have to make sure you look after it. After all, as the saying goes, 'you are what you eat' and if you just eat hamburgers then you just might end up looking like one!

History is a good mapping device of learning from other times and cultures. In the United Kingdom the health of the nation was never better than when food was rationed in the Second World War.[23] Why is that? Refined sugar was not readily available, processed food was not part of the diet, therefore obesity did not exist. People were walking or cycling to work. The work was manual and there was more physical activity, rather than sitting at a computer all day. Sometimes, I only count around 3,000 to 4,000 steps a day, if I just sit at my desk and complete computer work all day without doing any physical exercise. According to research by Global Corporate Challenge (GCC) and the employee health and performance programme, you are meant to do more than 10,000 steps a day to keep yourself on the right track to staying healthy. To do 10,000 steps every day takes commitment, and is an excellent habit to maintain; although I must confess I cannot do this every day if I am travelling by car for a few hours a day.

Choices in your education

This is a good investment, as it can be connected to your well-being and opening up your options and horizons for the future. A good education can help you to succeed in life, meet interesting people who can connect you with other people that can help enhance your progress at a much quicker rate than starting from the bottom. I am not saying that you cannot succeed in life if you did not end up at a leading public school – not at all. However, making time and the right choices in your education for yourself and children could prevent you and your family being disadvantaged.

Personally, my advanced education came much later in life. As a family, when I was younger, we were always on the move as my dad received promotions with the bank. Whilst moving from school to school, with different education experiences, I did not take to school when I was younger. One of the reasons for this was that when I was living in Hereford in the early 70s, the local school introduced a new experimental education system called the Initial Teaching Alphabet (ITA) designed by Sir James Pitman in the 60s, grandson of the inventor of Pitman shorthand. ITA consists of 42 letters, 24 standard lowercase Latin letters plus a number of special letters, most of which are modified Latin letters. This style of teaching in the 70s was very unhelpful and really slowed me and others down in our education.[24] However, I did go back into education seriously when I was much older. Those that return to education when they are advanced in years or have young families to provide for and look after, may find it harder to study, rather than when they are in their early teens and twenties when we have more time without the so-called distractions of life.

I do want to encourage you, the reader, to keep on continuing with education and studying to progress where your dreams are wishing to take you. Not everyone is cut out for university but there are apprenticeships and other forms of education to select from. Whichever path you take, your future is dependent on what investment you have taken. Needless to say, many university students are now in debt and may not be in the ideal role they hoped for when leaving university. However, they still have an education to help them on their way and they can utilise it in the future.

From my observations most countries are faced with two dilemmas: the need to advance and keep ahead of technology and progress to feed, heat and mobilise their ever-increasing populations; and then the need for a group of people who do not advance so much, to do the more menial jobs. Therefore each country may come up with plans to help control their population by dumbing down a certain amount of the population or groups of people, as each civilisation needs someone to do the jobs that nobody else wants to do, and control those individuals' income and expectations.

On the other hand, countries require well-educated people to help each country progress into the twenty-first century. Thomas L. Friedman identifies where modern countries have been neglecting the need to advance all their citizens.[25] However, some Western countries have been standing still too long and not advancing enough of their people. Friedman comments on how the scientists at NASA have been the same group of people for many years and many of them now are ready for retirement. NASA has commented that they have not been able to encourage enough of the younger generation to come forward. The book suggests that this 'Y Generation' has had it too easy with everything they needed at their fingertips in their bedrooms and not looking for work in NASA or similar organisations.

To help us understand the Y Generation better, Randall S. Hansen PhD, has written an article where he explains the perception of the Y Generation as being lazy, as they have learned to surf the net, but not done the deep-dive research in books that provided the top line information on the web.[26] Generation Y is about enjoying life first, not work. It has little respect for authority, is too self-centred and individualistic. Generation Y have unrealistic expectations as they want to work in coffee shops that have a 'hip vibe' or are more social and relaxed, rather than working in an office or systematic institution environment. NASA is all about security, scientific secrecy working from within NASA and applying the grey cells and the hard work of deep-dive research. Therefore NASA may have to look at bringing in more hard-working intelligent people from other countries, such as India and China. The West has been getting it wrong for some time. Dumbing down their people, allowing so called 'developing countries' that have clearly been advancing in science, mathematics and advanced computer technologies to come to the fore.

Without a doubt, we are all born with different abilities and some will thrive on education and some will run from it. I would like to encourage you to continue learning and developing even in your later years. Technology is increasing at an exponential rate, so we need to be able to keep pace of the ever-increasing inventions. In fact, God encourages us to study spiritually[27] and therefore we should not neglect our general studies too. We have no alternative but to establish and continue our personal development.

God is interested in our whole well-being, so selecting a good training course is a good choice for the future and will outweigh the initial costs of funding the course. What we learn now will always help us in the future.

Additionally, I have discovered that reading the Bible frequently helps my personal education to be more productive because it is a springboard to enable the dreams and plans that are inside of me. Whilst we are on earth, we should remember that no-one wants to listen to a fool and what we put into our minds and hearts helps us and others to progress in the future.

Education can only help you and your family advance and open up yourself for greater things to come. Opportunities can be ignored due to ignorance or a lack of understanding as to how to utilise what is in your grasp.

Economics in the Scriptures

Over the last two decades I have noticed how some churches have adopted a love of prosperity and become fixated on the prosperity part of the Bible rather than the gospel message. Jesus is the good news that has the authority and power to forgive sins and teach us how to live correctly and spread the good news of the Kingdom of God.

We should remember what Paul the apostle (the older man) said to Timothy (the young preacher) regarding money: *'For the love of money is the root of all evil. While coveting after money, some have strayed from the faith and pierced themselves through with many sorrows.'*[28]

Money is not the root of all evil, but the love of it is. *'The protection of wisdom is like the protection of money.'*[29] So wisdom and money have a relationship that needs to be respected and dovetailed together. Money is the best defence from debt. Many people and churches are struggling from not having the finances to implement the plan of God in their local community. All churches need money to do things for the kingdom; we cannot neglect ourselves either. It may surprise you that Jesus talks about money more than baptism; there are over 800 references in the Bible about money matters. Jesus said, *'So if you have not been faithful in the unrighteous wealth, who will commit to your trust the true riches.'*[30]

In another scripture, Jesus uses the parable of the talents in the natural to talk about the things in the spiritual. Two of the three servants doubled their investment and experienced a Jubilee reward. Why was this? Simply, the servants looked, tried, developed, were productive, and thought to make something of the gift that their master had entrusted into their hands. The hard work paid off, as the two talents became four, and five talents became ten. All of the increase happened over a process of time, it was not overnight. Sometimes we want things to happen instantly and shy away from things when we do not see an instant result.

However, the lazy servant was afraid of advancing with his master and decided not to increase his gift but, instead, he buried his one talent. For me the scripture is clearly advising us not to bury our spiritual and natural talents; we should not expect to get something back if we have not used what we have been given. We have to work and be more productive within our spiritual life as well as our natural life to increase what God has started us off with.

To help me increase the money I had obtained so far, I found that I needed to make the money work for me, known as 'sweating the asset'. In the same way your spiritual talent only increases if you are not a lazy servant. I have known people who have an understanding of how money can work for them while they are asleep at night. Most people make money when they arrive at their work place but they may not be increasing what they have saved elsewhere, as the interest rate is so low. However, by taking a portion of their saved money and finding a better rate of interest or doing something else with another type of investment, or an Internet business, they may make further money while they are sleeping.

Is it wrong for Christians to be productive in the natural? Well from Abraham, Jacob and Daniel, to Joseph they were all extremely blessed in the natural and the spiritual. Jesus wishes us to love one another, help one another, bless one another. We cannot ignore that we still need to provide an inheritance for the next generation as well as being rich in God. Paul's trade was tent making,[31] which he would do as and when he travelled on his missions. This may not be seen as a high-powered job today, but in Paul's day tents were a very necessary requirement. Paul was doing something that was in demand to help provide funds and make a contribution to his needs.

Money and the economy of a country are constantly changing due to changes around the world: different trade winds such as the addiction to the latest new thing; dropping one commodity for another; government and political changes; wars or rumours of war; the groundswell of people thinking and moving or reacting in different ways. Why is this? They reallocate the money to a better investment e.g. different bank interest rate, investment in gold, the property market (which always seems to increase every seven years), shares, gilts, bonds, art, antiques, cars – the list goes on. These all have a place in the market for the wise investor.

We just need to be prepared to change our investments when the wind blows in another direction. The investors who may not change are potentially at risk of greater losses if they need to liquidate their current assets for some reason. I am suggesting it may be better to be open to moving your investment where the changes occur. Ecclesiastes[32] helps me to identify how to look at the potential risks and opportunities in life and use King Solomon's observations and wisdom to improve my understanding of my spiritual endeavours to progress as well as the practical financial need to provide for the family. My main point here is that we need to find a practical way to be productive so we have a means of providing for ourselves and our families and not have a mentality that we cannot progress or that we need to live as poor people.

We can also learn from other people and statistics that are in the public domain. In the news it has been widely reported that some people will have kept the same bank for the past twenty years or so, but may have changed their wife two or three times in that same time span. The loyalty that people have shown towards their first bank is amazing, and the banks are not always the best way to look after your investments. In fact when you weigh up how much the bank has charged you and given you back in interest over the same time as your years of marriage, then you will realise that to make good investments you need to be doing your homework and keep on checking where you are and what has happened over the years of the investment.

Giving back

Warren Buffet, the American businessman, investor and philanthropist, is the most successful investor of the twentieth century. He has been noted to provide six quotes to practically help anyone who is wishing to understand money better:

1. On Earnings: 'Never depend on a single income. Make investments to create a second source.'
2. On Spending: 'If you buy things you do not need, soon you will have to sell things you need.'
3. On Savings: 'Do not save what is left after spending, but spend what is left after saving.'
4. On Taking Risks: 'Never test the depth of a river with both feet.'

5. On Investments: 'Do not put all your eggs into one basket.'
6. On Expectations: 'Honesty is a very expensive gift. Do not expect it from cheap people.'

Warren Buffet is the third wealthiest man in the world, and he still lives in the same modest home that he bought 57 years ago in 1958 for $31,500. Surely we can learn some things about his modesty and understanding of how not to waste money, chasing the things perhaps we just do not need.

Giving back to the community is being taken on board by more business men and women and leaders in the twenty-first century, and becoming a growing trend in the business world and one that the church needs to continue to do.

Examples of people in the business world who continue to give to good causes:

- John Timpson – Chairman of Timpson shoe repairers, who is a profound philanthropist and author of Upside Down Management. John helps to provide jobs for ex-convicts.
- Richard Branson – for his charity work in South Africa and other countries.
- Bill Gates – for providing financial support, giving help and support for poorer nations with cheaper drugs and his encouragement to others to become philanthropic.
- Oprah Winfrey and Steven Spielberg both give generously to organisations that provide help to those in need.
- The late Diana, Princess of Wales is reported to have visited the homeless at night under the arches near the Embankment, on her way home to Buckingham Palace.

Another key biblical principle being highlighted here is success. Success can be measured in different ways: in monetary terms, education, completing or winning a race, or success may be in helping those in need people, providing you with purposeful life. *'He who gives to the poor will not lack, but he who hides his eyes will have many a curse.'*[33] Regardless of how you measure success, if you help the poor and people in need your success is secure.

Taking the Macedonian church as an example, they were in poverty, dealing with a great trial of affliction, they were hungry, and they were in great lack. Yet they were able to give to the ministry – so much so that they were able to support Titus and send him to save the wealthiest region of churches in Corinth. To top it all, they did it with joy. This goes against our usual human behaviour and may be one of the biggest moves of the Spirit of God in the New Testament early church age, following the Day of Pentecost,[34] involving people who had nothing. This was indeed a leap of faith and generosity, to give away what they had whilst having nothing in reserve.

The Word of God describes the actions of the Macedonians as *'beyond their means'*.[35] A total submission to God's will and work will allow God to take over and bless those that have not. These are the type of good choices I am describing and promoting in this book. Making choices rich in God's purpose for you and others. Good choices sustain your future for longevity and sustainability in the Lord; which is beyond our power.

Their deep poverty abounded unto the riches of their liberality. For some reason those that have nothing find it easier to give than those who have much.

Giving from a young age

There is no set age when a child understands about profit or increase, but what is important is the need to understand the value of making good choices to help them for the future, and to be able to give to the less fortunate. One of the keys to understanding the value of money is to teach people to spend less than what is received. In that way a child will discover surplus. If by chance a child requires more funds to make a purchase, then encourage the child to come up with creative ways to earn the extra; after all, money does not grow on trees and this is a good principle to learn. Have you ever noticed how a child spends their money? There are so many options. Do they spend all their pocket money on sweets, magazines, iTunes or treats rather than making a choice to invest the money into a savings account? Do they split their money into pockets for spending, saving and giving? Some children will save and not spend a penny, nor lend or give to any good cause. Is the child encouraged to tithe or give to charity? Hopefully they have picked up your best attributes as children often learn by example.

Let me provide an insight on how we are best to behave at a time of crisis. For me, the miracle within the miracle that gets unnoticed in the feeding of the five thousand,[36] where a young lad gave away not some but all of his lunch to Jesus. For this to have happened, I believe the boy must have had an encounter with God or received previous good grounding from his parents. For the lad to forego and sacrifice his lunch when he was just as exhausted and hungry as the multitude, is a miracle in itself. God must have been at work through the child since giving all you have goes against the natural behaviour of a young boy, even at the best or worst of times.

To love, share and think of others before themselves, often pays dividends to the financial strength of a person. The widow who gave away her last two pennies knew the importance of giving.[37] Just think of her reward in heaven.

My top tip would be to learn to map your family history: ask yourself whether some generations produced or achieved more or less than another generation? Why is this? I suggest you ask yourself what has made people in your family successful or not. Is it down to education, place of birth, your colour, luck? I would prefer to re-interpret luck as making your own chances and opportunities, hard work, determination and/or God's favour.

To help you start thinking and turning the tables on the past, why not start mapping out your natural and spiritual history, the choices that have been made in your parents' and grandparents' lives. What has worked well for them and you?

How do you control cashflow in your practical life? Do you find that you buy food rather than make things yourself? Are you able to live within your means? Are you able to spend less than you earn. Are you investing/saving some of your earnings for the future? Or are you finding that you just do not have enough money to cover the bills. By focusing on your current accounts, you can see trends of spending that may be curved to a better direction for the future.

Endnotes
1. Genesis 8:22
2. Genesis 1:11,12,29
3. Genesis 1:24
4. Genesis 1

5. A *double-dip recession* is when gross domestic product (GDP) growth slides back to negative
6. Ecclesiastes 3:1
7. Genesis 37:3–11
8. Genesis 39:1–20
9. Hebrews 13:5
10. Genesis 39:20–23
11. Genesis 40:5–15
12. Genesis 41:37–44
13. Galatians 6:7
14. Luke 8:50
15. Matthew 19:26
16. Psalm 24:1
17. Genesis 2:15
18. Acts 16:1–4
19. Ecclesiastes 9:4
20. Joshua 14:12
21. *Journal of American Medicine (JAMA)* 2011–2012
22. Type 2 diabetes mellitus: 'the silent killer' *Practical Diabetes International* Volume 8, issue 6 July/August 2001. Ian W. Campbell FRCP, Consultant Physician, Victoria Hospital, Kirkcaldy, and Honorary Professor. Article first published online: 5 September 2001. See also http://www.preventtype2.org/what-is-diabetes.php
23. Adam Smith Institute, 'The joys of food rationing, the perils of obesity', Tim Warstall, 10 January 2015
24. omniglot.com/writing/ita.htm
25. Thomas L. Friedman, *The World is Flat*, (2005)
26. Randall S. Hansen PhD, 'Perceptions Vs Reality: 10 Truths About Generation Y Workforce'
27. 2 Timothy 2:15
28. 1 Timothy 6:10
29. Ecclesiastes 7:12
30. Luke 16:11
31. Acts 18:3
32. Ecclesiastes chapter 11
33. Proverbs 28:27
34. Acts 2
35. 2 Corinthians 8:1–7

36. John 6:9
37. Mark 12:41–44

2
Do Your Homework
(Preparation is the Key to Success)

Homework is one of those words that can send shudders of anxiety through individuals. I never liked doing homework when I was at school because I had more interesting things to do, like watching TV. My strategy was clear: to complete any homework before I got home and take advantage of the TV schedule. I managed to do this by finishing my homework in the lunch break, obtaining the relevant information from my school friends or, more risky still, doing the homework in another lesson.

I now know that I would have done much better at school if I had found the best learning environment possible and not cheated myself on the full learning experience. What we may have gotten away with in the past is not best practice for our long-term outlook. When we short change or cheat on the time we provide for ourselves to learn we do ourselves harm and learn to plagiarise, rather than learn off our own back and find out things for ourselves.

A change of strategy is required to gain better results and achieve more. In the example with my homework, I did the minimum to complete my homework and my goal was to watch

TV. But if my focus had been on learning, I would have taken greater care over my homework and achieved better results. What I have found out through the University of Life is that most of my success is based on 90 per cent homework: the more research and investigation that is done behind the scenes the better. This means, less time spent watching the TV! I now treat homework as a good choice with a positive outcome later on down the road. I now think of homework as research. One of the tools of research that I prefer to use is 'mapping': looking at past events to see what we can learn and utilise for the future.

Mapping

I use mapping in all sorts of ways in the Word of God to identify patterns of behaviour, such as identifying comparisons between Isaac and Jesus who had many similar experiences; for tracking journeys such as Paul's, and what he went through to set up churches all around Europe. I use it for linking scriptures that are connected across the Old and New Testament. At work we use mapping to track all sorts of activity: to identify progress with sales, value creation, service levels and key performance indicators or a reduced amount of complaints. Hopefully, over time, we will be able to identify trends that will be helpful to exploit or find corrective action.

Do you know why people join or leave the church we attend? If you were able to track the trends, then perhaps the church would be better placed to keep people-retention levels higher for longer and attract more people. Mapping can be used to identify missing information also known as 'gap analyses'. Following a series of quantitative and qualitative questions, which have been answered, any gaps in process or service requirements can be resolved with further work activities. Once I have identified the gaps, I know I will need to come up with a strategy to improve the current situation and be more productive.

Mapping cannot predict the future, but can be an effective tool to learn from history or to provide insights of up-and-coming trends.

Fred Harrison's property cycle is something you can find on the Internet to help you understand the property market; it's geared for the West.[1] This is not an exact science, but by mapping previous trends you will be able to understand the property market better. Cycle 18 theory has predicted years in advance the last three 'boom and bust' peaks and troughs by understanding the 18-year property cycle. Harrison has mapped the UK housing cycle for the past 232 years. Harrison's method of predicting the trends of when it is a good time to buy and sell is referred to as 14 years of increase, followed by 4 years of depression when houses become unaffordable. The spirit of greed helped to inflate the last few years of the cycle, or any latecomer, naïve of the market being inflated, paying the asking price without any means to negotiate or wait for the price to come down.

Let's look at a project that you wish to map (track). First of all, identify the items to include in your project and the current state of each item (i.e. started, completed, delayed or in progress), and identify if you or others in your group are happy with the progress. Once you have identified the 'gaps' then make any additional decisions to complete the tasks. Before I enter anything new, I always weigh up the pros and cons to assess the viability of a commercial project. Sometimes our emotions overwhelm our ability to think and evaluate clearly. To be able to make good choices and decisions in life we need to be able to sift all the chaff (rubbish) at the beginning of the selection process or allow a time during the selection process where we can make informed choices and decisions.

In Josh Kaufman's book *The Personal MBA*, he has a formula to see if something is viable. I have made a few tweaks to this model and suggest putting a score of one to ten (ten is high for excellent). I suggest that if you score over 75 per cent then the project is worth looking at. Furthermore, only get involved in projects that you have some knowledge and passion about. In other words, do not open a restaurant if you do not understand food, you are not able to cook or you are not prepared to work long, unsociable hours. Remember, not everything that sparkles is gold, therefore not everything that comes your way will be right for you; what works for one person, might not work for you. If we self-manufacture dreams as we may be persuaded to by copying someone else's idea, ministry or project that looks to be successful, then we could be starting out on an adventure where we never find 'our groove' and living a life that we may not be enjoying or being purposeful to the extent that God intended for us. I believe our dreams, aspirations and innovations come from God. Applying some homework at the beginning might just help us start off on the right track and avoid years of disillusionment. Try out the following practical tool to see if this helps you make the next good choice in your natural life. The questions would need to be adjusted for the spiritual as the commercial emphases are less important.

Viable model

Ask yourself these questions and answer them truthfully.

Urgency: How badly do people need this right now?

Market size: How many people would purchase this?

Pricing potential: What's the highest price people would be willing to pay?

Cost of customer acquisition: How easy is it to acquire a new customer?

Cost of value delivery: How much does it cost to create and deliver the offer?

Uniqueness of offer: How unique is your offer versus that of the competition? How easy is it to copy?

Speed to market: How quickly can you create and sell?

Up-front investment: How much do you have to invest before having an offer ready?

Up-selling potential: What related offers could you present to purchasing customers?

Evergreen potential: Once the offer is created, how much work do you have to put into it to continue selling?

Total:

Further questions to consider:

How attractive is the market for your idea?

Can you alter the idea to appeal to a more attractive market?

This is where, at times, the heart (the emotions) and the head (the mind) can be separated from each other, when you need to be able to have harmony between your head and heart. Additionally, as Christians we have the Spirit of God dwelling within us, therefore we have to keep all three on track and in alignment. This is where mapping can help you decide what choices to make because a map helps you decide what route to take. All of this guidance will help you to plan ahead. We do need to be prepared to ask ourselves some questions, just as the man that built something to last for a long time. Ask yourself: do I have the staying power, commitment, sustainability to complete the project? *'For who among you, intending to build a tower, does not sit down first and count the cost to see whether he has resources to complete it?'*[2]

When I think of taking on a project I tend to think of Ecclesiastes 11, as it helps me to be prepared for anything that life might throw my way. We can look at this scripture in the natural and the spiritual sense. It encourages me, like a life-line, to have a direct connection with God. I can hear him and feel him with the rest of the angels in heaven, saying keep going, apply yourself again to the task in hand, especially when I am facing tough choices or challenges in my working day and in my spiritual life. It helps me to remember to maintain a balance and perspective on life. Things do happen in life that we are not expecting. Bad things do happen as well as the blessings that we are privileged to receive.

In my lifetime the world has certainly changed since the attack on the Twin Towers in 2001. We have to be prepared for things to go randomly wrong. The scripture encourages us to make an extra effort to succeed in whatever we are called to do. You may face exceptional spiritual and natural attacks on your faith, home, work, family and church environment. There are no God-given dreams, promises and destinies where you will not experience bumps in the road as you carry on your life's journey. There are lots of choices in life to undertake and there will be many crossroads and distractions to overcome. But stay focused on what you are called to do.

The calling of God will burn inside of you; it will be more than a faint awakening. What we must not do is ignore our God-given talents, gifts, requests for help and what God is calling us to do. It does not matter what people say, or what hindrances come at the beginning; just keep going. I would say if you do get feedback, and sometimes feedback can be harsh or not welcomed, then do listen to what someone might be saying. It might just be the advice you need to help you trim the rough diamond you started out as, before you are transformed into something amazing.

Just like Simon who, I think, represents humanity, the old nature of man in the Gospels, Jesus called Simon (meaning 'reed like') and then later renamed him Peter ('the rock'). Simon was like a rough diamond who Jesus called to follow him, way before anyone would ever recognise the great leadership qualities that Peter would be able to demonstrate later on in the book of Acts and the two letters he wrote in the New Testament. Peter demonstrates what a Christian, a new person in Christ, can aspire to.

The transformation of Simon-Peter was a whole, life-long project for Jesus. Peter was totally transformed by learning and being with Jesus for three-and-a-half years or so. The transformation process takes time to mature and materialise. All we need to do is be practical, be patient with ourselves and others (we are all rough diamonds) as it is a process to shape a beautiful gem. We will start out as novices in the natural and be transformed into spiritual, amazing Christians if time allows, which is beyond our means and natural thinking ability. We have to learn to trust in God.

With Simon we can reflect and map out his journey and the choices he made. Peter, later in life, became the perfect Christian example for us all. Simon was transformed into Cephas the rock, from being this shaky, reed-like person (Simon), an impetuous, rash, hot-headed and sometimes reckless fisherman from Galilee, to being transformed into a solid pillar within the new church generation; a shining beacon, an apostle of Jesus, who would later stand up on the day of Pentecost and preach to a multitude of 3000 people, turning their hearts back to God, just as Joel had prophesied way back in the Old Testament. My hairs stand up on the back of my neck with excitement when I think how Peter changed.

Carrying on with this thought from Ecclesiastes, I can simultaneously identify with what King Solomon is writing about relating to our faith in God, about the things that we cannot see and that there might be good times as well as destruction around the corner, as well as applying oneself to go further and the need to invest more time or funds into your project. To be clear, when I am talking about investing, I am not always referring to monetary value. It could be spending time with loved ones or people needing my help, or studying for a new qualification. Ecclesiastes advises us all to *'Give a portion to seven, or even eight, for you do not know what calamity may happen on the earth'*.[3]

My experience in life is that not every seed planted produces fruit. Some seeds do not grow, while others take hold and are able to spread. The scripture encourages us to be generous when sowing and suggests seven to eight times, rather than just one seed. In practical terms, some of my projects have not started off well, before I saw a return or reward or accomplishment on the original thought, choice or investment. Sometimes I receive a return on my investment (ROI) and I am able to pay myself back the start-up costs as well as reap some profit, 'the spoils'. Some people may give up too soon at the point where they do not receive an immediate return on their invested resources, whether they have invested in church or in a business.

Their single seed approach may not have worked out for them the first time round so they turn away from their original dream as they did not sow, plant, work, pray more than the one time. Sometimes a project fails and the original dream is lost, with no return. This is when an individual may feel discouraged because they have lost out on their first or new adventure. However, experience tells me to be prepared for the adverse and not to rely on a one-time activity seed or project to see a healthy, productive outcome.

In the natural it goes without saying that if you are thinking of going into business or seeking an investment opportunity you should be prepared to lose money at some point within the early stages of the business, and realise that it takes faith to plan and to press on through when you are losing money. Solomon advises that it takes many days to see a return when you cast your bread on the water, and sometimes – as previously mentioned – calamity may come and destroy some of what you have hoped for.

Simultaneously, in the spiritual it goes without saying, if you are answering the call and thinking of going into ministry or seeking to do something for God and to be a witness, be prepared that things might not go the way you planned at some point within the early stages of the journey.

Allow me to introduce further practical and spiritual examples that we can observe from scripture. One of the lessons to learn from the story and experiences of Joseph is to think about the future, so we are able to supply for the needs of others. It is all about planning and preparing for the future in faith, even though we do not know what is around the corner. Joseph was given the insight from God that there was a famine forthcoming after a time of blessing. Joseph had the gift from God to be able to interpret Pharaoh's dream of seven prosperous years and seven years of famine.

I feel this is where the West may have gone wrong in the decade from 1998 to 2008; they did not save or spend their money wisely. So when the recession hit in 2008, there were insufficient funds to relieve the 'famine', which turned out to be a double-dip recession in close succession. Remember, our seasons are cyclic: summer, autumn, winter, spring, and we should aim for contentment – which I know is easier to say than do, but harder to manage when the times are unpredictable. When things are going well, whether naturally or spiritually, we need to be constantly planning for the next generation and what they need to survive any onslaughts.

Let's look at some spiritual trends (mapping) when Israel (God's chosen people) found themselves in trouble or captivity in Egypt or Babylon. What insights can we glean?

If we follow the messianic line from Abram to align ourselves with the blessings of God – *'and in you all families of the earth will be blessed*[4] – the Bible refers to Isaac as the chosen son of Abraham and Isaac's son was Jacob, whose name God changed to Israel. Israel had twelve sons who found themselves in Egypt due to a harsh famine. In Exodus 1 we read the names of Israel's sons who entered Egypt with Jacob (Israel). We note that all the twelve tribes of Israel found themselves in bondage. Additionally, in Exodus 1 we find Israel being held in captivity and oppressed in Egypt, with a new king in authority who did not know Joseph and governed harshly against Israel, as this new king of Egypt feared this growing community of God-fearing people. The story gets even worse for Israel as the new cruel, superstitious, idol-worshipping Pharaoh whipped and tried to stop the people of Israel worshipping the true living God: *'Therefore they set taskmasters over them to afflict them with their labour. They built for Pharaoh storage cities: Pithom and Rameses.'*[5]

This oppression lasted for many years. I am sure if I was living at that time and under that harsh regime, I would be wondering where was this blessing that Abram was talking about? I might be complaining and asking questions too, about when I might be able to see and feel the blessings of the Lord: 'When will I be able to live my own life and be free to enjoy the adventures of life?'

Then we find in Exodus an encouraging text; buried between all that cruelty, turmoil and distress, a ray of hope, which I personally refer to when things are not going to plan in the way that I hoped for. Out of extreme pain, hardship, anguish and oppression, God's people can and will prosper: *'But the more they afflicted them, the more they multiplied and grew so that as a result they abhorred the sons of Israel.'*[6]

This quote from Israel's history is one of the keys to our

Christian success today. God blesses you in times of distress. Nothing can separate us from the love of God, even in times of annihilation and ethnic cleansing. Against all odds Israel grew into a great nation while in captivity. So much so, that when Israel left Egypt they were about two- to five-million strong. We should never take things for granted, for God does always take care of his people. Therefore we need to praise and worship God at all times. The way God wishes his people to be blessed may be via a different path than we would wish to choose, but God is sovereign in all sickness, life experiences, dreams, our best made action plans, self-limitations and, even if we fall into sin to any degree, God has his ways to save us and bless us.

As we look into the New Testament I notice the book of Acts mapping across Israel's history.[7] Let's see what happens to Israel following the 430 years of bondage. Moses led the Israelites out of Egypt and Egypt gave them gold and silver and precious items with which to leave Egypt. Israel left Egypt a very wealthy nation by a transfer of wealth orchestrated by God. Israel got as far as the Red Sea with Pharaoh's army pursuing them. Moses had a choice: be delivered into the hands of the army or follow God's instruction. Moses pointed his staff at the Red Sea, and the sea opened enabling Israel to cross on dry land. The book of Exodus goes on to inform us that as the Egyptian army pursued Israel they were destroyed as the Red Sea rolled back. God is in control of your situation. God provided the Law to Moses at Mount Sinai to provide governance to his people and even in the forty years of wilderness God provided manna from heaven to feed his people. When Moses died, God provided another leader: Joshua. Joshua led Israel to claim the Promised Land.

As we take our journey into the twenty-first century, we may face invasion, captivity, bondage, but God will always open up a door to save his people. God can create an escape route out of anything for his people.

We can learn a tremendous amount from the captivity of the four Hebrew boys. They had tenacity, they were free from fear and trusted simply and solely in God. The Kingdom of Israel was divided into two states: the northern kingdom (ten tribes) of Israel was taken into captivity in Assyria;[8] and the southern kingdom (Judah), consisting of the tribes of Judah and Benjamin, were taken into Babylon for seventy years.[9] Nebuchadnezzar destroyed and laid waste Jerusalem and its temple. But even in Babylon, the four Hebrew boys found favour. Here are some observations of how the four boys were ten times better than the Babylonians in a hostile environment.[10]

These four children found themselves in captivity of Babylon by the king and ruler Nebuchadnezzar. Their whole life was turned upside down, their personal plans scuppered, their homes, friends, relations all gone. These boys had dreams and aspirations as many young people have. They knew and worshipped Jehovah, yet they were caught up in this invasion. When you find yourself uprooted from your home and then re-planted in some other country and barbaric culture, the simple things in life, like home-cooked food, are now only a distant memory and off the menu. Without a doubt their whole personality could have changed. They could have adopted an aggressive manner, rebelled against God or become ring leaders to start a revolt. But they remained faithful to God.

Their names were changed to erase their birth names and the

new names given contradicted their original Hebrew names:

- Daniel, which means 'judge of God', was renamed Belteshazzar, meaning Bela, a Babylon god.
- Hananiah, which means 'Jah has favoured', was renamed Shadrach, meaning doubtful.
- Mishael, which means 'what God is', was renamed Meshach which means Babylon god.
- Azariah, which means 'Jah has helped', is now called Abednego which is, in part, a Babylon god.

The names Shadrach, Meshach and Abednego roll off the tongue smoothly but the change of names was aimed at taking away their birth rights, their connection and references to Jehovah and Jerusalem.

Nebuchadnezzar remarked on their wisdom which is why they were handpicked. These four boys stood out because they were thriving under the pressure. God was blessing his faithful servants to make them shine in the face of the adversary.

An insight to wisdom is outlined in the opening chapters of Daniel. Simply, for wisdom to flow, you need the capacity to apply the qualities you have regardless of the environment around you. A wise person's action is consistent with their beliefs.

We lose creditability with God when we say one thing and do another. We have to create our own spiritual atmosphere regardless of the circumstances and where we find ourselves. *'If any of you lacks wisdom, let him ask of God, who gives to all men liberally and without criticism, and it will be given to him.'*[11]

Daniel then provides insight into the heart of man and how

powerful he can be when he has made up his mind.

'But Daniel purposed in his heart that he would not defile himself with the portion of the king's food, nor with the wine which he drank. Therefore he requested of the master of the officials that he might not defile himself.'[12]

Daniel knew the meat was sacrificed to idols and, as such, the decision he made was life-changing with death being a real outcome.

- In Daniel we see strong leadership in good and not so good times.
- The Hebrew boys were a strong team that showed loyalty regardless of the times and conditions.
- As four young people, they purposed in their hearts that they would not defile themselves.

Interestingly, King Nebuchadnezzar invested in the Hebrew boys, not wishing to keep with his own people. But he identified that these young men were talented and gifted. King Nebuchadnezzar realised these four boys still needed training and he provided a royal apprenticeship for them. We should never underestimate how important training is. Making choices about your continued education and investing in yourself, regardless of the situation, may mean sometimes making some important choices, between not having something in the here-and-now, but being prepared to wait until you have the natural and spiritual education that will enable you to move forward and be more industrious. I am sure your next training session will help you in your next promotion. *'Iron sharpens iron.'*[13]

Apply training to your heart and you will be equipping yourself and others around in the right direction to go up another level. Perhaps the following will encourage you to seek out what God wants you to be trained in next.

The king recognised that these four boys were ten times better than all his magicians, astrologers and wise men. The way man measures things is totally different to the way God measures things. Hopefully, now we can start to identify that man's ways are not God's way. See Chapter 5 later in the book.

Man tends to measure things in five different ways:

- By length (how long is the boundary around your house?)
- By mass (how heavy was the baby when it was born?)
- Temperature (how hot or cold is it?)
- Time (how short or how long is the church service?)
- Volume (how much fuel does your car hold, what size engine?)

You would be amazed how often we use these measurements to gauge ourselves and others or something we have seen, especially if someone is not content with themselves or lacks confidence. We are constantly contrasting and comparing in our minds when we notice something. From how we introduce ourselves to each other, how they look, birth order in families, height, weight, if we use notes or don't need notes when teaching or preaching, how we dress, professions, what a person's spouse does, other people's children, their car, their house – the list goes on.

As we know, *'Truthfully, I perceive that God is no respecter of persons.'*[14]

Whatever 'man measurement' you wish to measure yourself

with, do not beat yourself up if you have not achieved something by a certain age or time period. God wants to break up your human materialist expectation as God sees us for who we are in our hearts, rather than how tall we are or what is in our bank balance. We will all become something in the Lord if we are willing to put some preparation and hard work into our ministries.

When God told Samuel to go to Jesse's house, his mission was to anoint the next king of Israel. *'But the LORD said to Samuel, "Do not look on his appearance or on the height of his stature, because I have rejected him. For the LORD sees not as man sees. For man looks on the outward appearance, but the LORD looks on the heart."'* [15]

As I see it, David did not really fit in with his family.

David's birth order happened to be the youngest of all his older brothers; he was right at the back of the pecking order in his family. He was the smallest and, because he looked after the sheep, he was the smelliest and worst-dressed brother. David was outside in the field, he was not even considered worthy to receive an invite. He was ruddy-looking and in his family's eyes he was not fit for the anointing or to meet the prophet of the Lord.

It is not where you live, nor your age, nor height, nor your degrees, nor your fashion sense. Why did David wear those lion-skinned shoes and that bear coat? They don't even match! But they are his rewards and testimonies of his preparation in the field – training. David had been preparing to fight for his life from a very young age. David's heart was already in the right place to receive the anointing to be the next king of Israel, even though he had not met Goliath or maybe had not even heard of him. David had been practising to be able to stand on his own two feet, a good protector of the sheep, a leader and a man of God. Whilst he was in the mountains on his own he had learnt to feed, protect and lead the sheep.

David may have had primitive tools to work with – a sling and some small pebbles – but I am sure David had learnt to have a relationship with God in prayer, to be able to discern that there was a fox or a jackal on the prowl. David already found that he had something inside of himself that was not of his means or own strength or ability to stop the enemy in their tracks, no matter how wild the beast was. Likewise, it is what is inside of you and what you are really made of which counts for God. Nobody needs to have recognised or seen what you have done in the field. If we have been practising and preparing to enable us to find God's purpose in our hearts today, then God can use you in any type of situation in the future. Our time comes when we are willing to stand up for Christ.

How to be ten times better God's way

Daniel identified two main things to be ten times better than anyone else in his day: to have purpose in our hearts and the readiness to train for the king's table.

The number ten means trial or test. Just like the tithe is a test of our faith in God to help support the ministry. To give a tithe is God's measurement of how faithfulness should be. In the book of Daniel, when the four boys, Daniel, Hananiah, Mishael and Azariah, agreed not to defile themselves with the portion of the king's meat and wine, this was their first spiritual test.[16]

The boys had to eat pulses and drink water for ten days. The four boys got past their first test of not eating the king's meat and drinking the king's wine. Their appearance was noted by Melzar and they were presented to king Nebuchadnezzar.

Following this, a bigger test was to follow.[17] The three boys Hananiah, Mishael and Azariah, did not bow to Nebuchadnezzar's graven image. So, the three boys were bound and additional clothing was tied to their person, the fire was heated to seven-times hotter than normal, so much so the guards died from the heat before the three boys entered the fire. Note that at this time in their trial their leader, Daniel, was not with them. Where was Daniel? Your pastor might not always be physically with you in the fiery test (the test might be a tight situation that you may find yourself in), but Jesus is always right in the midst of the problem with you, if you invite him into the situation. God gives us something in reserve for our faith; that is great faith, which is not naturally present until God provides the back-up we need to win and survive the battle. A spiritual encounter with God occurs when we stand up and fight for him. He provides the means that is beyond our power.

The fire may get seven times hotter, but the boys were ten times better than any situation that was put in front of them. This was all down to them understanding their purpose and their willingness to be used by God to be a witness of his power, allowing them to withstand the evil devices of the enemy without fear.

Endnotes

1. http://thepropertypodcast.com/2014/07/tpp069-the-18-year-property-cy-cle/
2. Luke 14:28

3. Ecclesiastes 11:2
4. Genesis 12:1–3
5. Exodus 1:11
6. Exodus 1:12
7. Acts 7
8. 2 Kings 17
9. 2 Kings 25
10. Daniel 1
11. James 1:5
12. Daniel 1:8
13. Proverbs 27:17
14. Acts 10:34
15. 1 Samuel 16:7
16. Daniel 1
17. Daniel 3

3

Practical Understanding of Money and Spiritual Investments

⌒

Talking about money within the church environment can at times feel awkward. It is like 'the elephant in the room' – a subject that nobody wishes to talk about for fear of seeming to be focused on commercial aspirations, and being criticised of preaching prosperity.

However, without finances buildings close, ministries can be inhibited, people may not get fed spiritually and physically. It is interesting to note that it was a rich man, Joseph of Arimathea,[1] who rescued the crucified and beaten body of Jesus from being thrown to the dogs or burned. Joseph was a disciple of Jesus. It is good to know that it is possible to live for God and get the balance right for those that have to maintain a job or business, without being focused only on the money. It is this practical mature balance that I wish to encourage and highlight within this chapter.

As Christians we do need to be able to financially plan for the future, so that we have a constant flow of income in the pipeline to look after our family and the ministry that they attend.

Running a church or being part of the ministry is, in my view, one of the hardest jobs in the world to get right. This is why you really do need to be called by God to lead and look after people, as in Chapter 2. Making the right choices and decisions about money and future finances, like pension schemes or preparing for the future, should be discussed up front, as well as the love of God and other key messages in the Bible. Let's take a look at two different households. One household has complete openness and transparency, and all matters are discussed together as a family. The other household is more reserved and less open to discuss things that matter.

In the household where they have complete openness and maturity to discuss important matters, the parents have written out their wills and provided guidance notes to their family on what should happen if they were to pass away. The family that has discussed this in advance of anything happening may run more harmoniously than a family who never discusses the important finances and well-being of the parents.

Bringing this example closer to church, people need to be encouraged to understand how the ministry is funded and the importance of contributing to the church, so both will benefit the church, the work of God and the people of God.

The balance is not always easy to get right, but by not bringing the matter to the attention of the congregation and community there is the risk of individuals remaining in poverty when practical guidance can alleviate them from their situation.

Both Dale Carnegie (1888–1955) and Abraham Maslow (in Maslow's hierarchy of needs developed in 1943) identified that money was the fourth most important need of humans.

Even though we cannot take money to heaven with us, we can leave an inheritance for our family and church (see

Chapter 7 regarding inheritance). Being a Christian does not stop us from paying our way and being able to provide for others. Like the Good Samaritan, it is quite the opposite, as Jesus' parable demonstrated, it was the correct balance of love, care and providing for a complete stranger.[2]

Therefore, I believe we have to consider the need for balanced finances within the church and its membership, as something to get practically and spiritually right.

There is an old saying: 'Money makes the world go round' and, as such, money may always feature on our list of needs. Here is an example of some of the most common needs that Dale Carnegie and Maslow identified at different times:

1. Health and the preservation of life
2. Food
3. Sleep
4. Money and the things money can buy
5. Life in the hereafter
6. Sexual gratification
7. The well-being of our children
8. A feeling of importance

Each of these needs requires a certain amount of time and investment. The *Oxford Dictionary* provides the following definition of investments:

- Laying out money or capital in an enterprise with the expectation of profit.
- Or the commitment of something other than money (time,

energy or effort) to a project with the expectation of some worthwhile result.

To be expectant of receiving a return on investment means a seed has been planted months, if not years, in advance. You cannot expect to reap a harvest if you have not sown any seeds. Whilst not impossible, the reality is that we do not get something out of nothing.

Good investments or choices are part of life's choices. I am sorry, but there are no flashing neon lights saying: 'this is the right investment'; 'this is the right career for you'; 'this is the right spouse for you'. We all have to make choices in life that we do not know the final outcome of, or whether it is the right road to travel. We have to be confident to know when God is showing us something, or speaking to us because he wishes to guide us to our purpose.

Not everything that shines is gold. If it sounds too good to be true – when it is a money-related opportunity – be very careful! Do your homework and check things out.

For every investment, there is an element of *risk* associated to it. We can reduce the risk by doing our homework, as identified in the previous chapter. Once we have identified the possibilities and narrowed down the risk, we could then say there is a measured risk before we make some final choices.

In Chapter 1 I spoke about Solomon and how he recognised that 'money is a defence' for those who understand how to use it. In the New Testament, Paul wrote to young Timothy advising him that the love of money is a root of all evil for those that love it. Money in itself is fine; we have not lost our soul if we are blessed in that area. It is the love of money we need to stay away from and find a balance to avoid focusing on greed. Money can either be a help or a downfall. God will supply our needs not our greed.

Perhaps the key is to focus on contentment. If we are content, there is an inward peace which subtly draws satisfaction rather than greed.

King Solomon provides some guidance on how we should focus ourselves: *'Do not labour to be rich; cease from your own wisdom'*,[3] and in the book of Luke chapter 12 we read the parable of the rich man who was a fool to build bigger barns for himself. We learn that the rich man did not consult God with his plans; it was a self-manufactured desire. This example of the rich man helps us to utilise prayer to the maximum as it provides us access to God and we can consult him with our ideas to see if they are of God or of ourselves. Sometimes we do dream up things which are not of God. If we humble ourselves we can always curb our ideas or have a godly vision to implement them. *'Trust in the Lord with all your heart, and lean not on your own understanding.'*[4]

God encourages us to be generous and stretch our faith and try our hand at many things. We will never know if something will work for us unless we try to scatter the Word of God, just as an investor will invest in many things. An investor will have many strategies, from safe to high risk. Some of those investment strategies will work and may provide a thirty, sixty or hundred fold increase. Therefore, the same principles that we understand about sowing and reaping in faith to win souls for Jesus, are very similar in the natural too. In the natural we sow into investing time and effort into projects; if we do nothing with the opportunities that come our way via God, we may miss the opportunity and we may stay in poverty or end up in poverty.

'There is one who scatters, yet increases; and there is one who withholds more than is right, but it leads to poverty.'[5]

The key to making good choices and investments is to continually put into a project, rather than just taking out of a project. The more we put in, the more we will get out. Innovation can always provide growth, and growth increases our investment or increases our productivity beyond our original expectation in the natural and the spiritual.

As we consider how to find contentment,[6] which is easier to talk about than to find or practise continually, contentment does not mean to stop and do nothing, but it encourages us to be relaxed and less up-tight in making choices to grow. *'For I have learned in whatever state I am to be content.'*[7]

Life is a journey. From time to time you might find yourself without a job, in debt or you have earned a promotion or are starting a new business. We will all have highs and lows in the spiritual and the natural, but wherever you find yourself be content. Do not stop or go backwards if things don't go the way you wish all of the time. Never forget that it may be for a season. So keep pressing forward and investing time spiritually into Jesus, by reading the Word and praying, and sometimes fasting if need be. Make time for God in your life, and seek to help others, in health, in study, in finance or whatever you are directed to do.

In the twenty-first century, I do struggle to determine how to describe what being rich really means or looks like. We seem to have a rich category which is ever growing, from Lottery winners to people receiving high rewards for their contribution to their work place. They may have many houses, a yacht valued at several millions of pounds, along with all the paraphernalia that goes with that lifestyle. They may have a good few million in the bank, sometimes billions – today's mega rich.

If someone is on a good salary or in a business with a healthy turnover and profit, we might say they are 'well off' because they have a luxurious house and a cool car. By comparison, if someone has very little and may only be able to afford to rent a house or be homeless even, we may see the house owner as being rich by comparison. How do I measure what wealth means? What does rich really mean today?

To help us find the answer, we can consider the Bible character Job. After all, he was the richest man in the Bible and God looked after him during his time of affliction and prosperity. I admire Job's persistence to continually pray for his family. Chapter 1 in Job implies his children were not praying for themselves. Was this because they experienced great wealth in their lives and no lack, and felt that they were okay because they had houses and banquets to attend? I am reminded that we should continue to pray, irrespective of our personal circumstances, remembering not to take God for granted.

So is the Word of God against the wealthy?

The rich man in the book of Luke[8] seemed to only be inwardly focused on himself, and did not share his wealth, or support or help someone in need. He saw and knew of Lazarus, as he was quick to try and order Lazarus about when he found himself not in heaven. Therefore God deals with the rich man's greedy spirit.

Riches can be seen as monetary value or riches in the Kingdom of God – the Kingdom of God being the good works combined with our faith in Jesus. If we keep investing spiritual and financial gifts into the Kingdom of God, we will become stronger and retain what we have originally been blessed with, and be better placed to pass on an inheritance either spiritually or financially – hopefully both.

Let me confirm that it is possible to be rich and powerful and be kind and generous at the same time. As mentioned earlier, it was the rich man, Joseph of Arimathea, who risked his life and went boldly to Pilate to ask for the body of Jesus. Jesus' disciples, Matthew, Mark, Peter and John, were nowhere to be seen. It took a wealthy man who was connected, who had stature, influence and purpose, to provide a proper burial for Jesus. Jesus was buried in a rich man's tomb, which was a new grave. Nobody else had previously been buried there and this was all provided by Joseph of Arimathea. It is good to be able to provide for the future, rather than leave the burden for someone else. When it came to the need, Joseph was able to give.

Understanding the value of money

I was not born into a family that was flush with money, but my dad did teach me the value of money. Let me share a very simple story with you. When I was around thirteen, if I dug the garden and cut the grass, I would receive something extra in my pocket money. Because I worked for the money, I did not squander it. But when I did spend it on something, I found my savings decreased. These episodes taught me that the value of money will decrease unless you are continually investing into your finances. We need to keep putting in, to keep topping up.

The book *Sudden Money* by Susan Bradley is helpful for anyone who wishes to understand this principle. Individuals who come into sudden money may find they blow the whole lot in a short space of time due to lack of knowledge about investment. A biblical example is the prodigal son who had a great time, but soon blew away his inheritance. When I was a child, the church taught me to save some, share some, put some aside to treat myself. It does not matter if you have a little or a lot. You can spread your investment across the church, yourself and the things that are needed. Your investments will be in God – (church and charity and people in need), your household and some for yourself. This is a simple principle to implement to see a good investment in all three key areas.

My top ten principles to understand how investments can help people through the Scriptures

The following list is my suggested top ten principles (in no particular order) governed by God's Word and our attitude to life's choices in investments. God's reward to his people only happens if the principles have been implemented. The biggest reward will be in heaven, but there is no reason why Christians cannot be blessed while on earth. The first four are reflective of what the Macedonian churches did for the Corinthian church. Paul was so grateful for their gratitude and he provides the spiritual and practical insights and benefits of giving in love. As Paul said, 'the Macedonians supplied'; none of the other churches were mentioned.

1. *'But this I say: He who sows sparingly will also reap sparingly,*

and he who sows bountifully will also reap bountifully.[9] The key principle here is our attitude towards giving whether it may be financial or acts of kindness.

2. *'Let every man give according to the purposes in his heart, not grudgingly or out of necessity, for God loves a cheerful giver.'*[10] When we give, we need to give cheerfully.

3. *As it is written: "He has dispersed abroad, He has given to the poor; His righteousness remains forever."'*[11] God is not complicated; let us not hold back our hand to the people in need.

4. *'Now He who supplies seed to the sower and supplies bread for your food will also multiply your seed sown and increase the fruits of your righteousness.'*[12] We need to bless the sower. Jesus is the sower, as is the pastor who we sit under in church.

5. *'Give, and it will be given to you: Good measure, pressed down, shaken together, and running over will men give unto you. For with the measure you use, it will be measured unto you.'*[13] This scripture is self-explanatory. God gives back to us more than we give to others.

6. *'Do not labour to be rich; cease from your own wisdom.'*[14] I know we have to work to earn money to live. However, our focus should not be only on the money, but rather on our contribution to the company or organisation that we work for. We should look for job satisfaction rather than financial reward, because we may never be satisfied if we focus on the money.

7. *'There is one who scatters, yet increases; and there is one who withholds more than is right, but it leads to*

poverty.'[15] This verse encourages us to continue to look for ways spiritually and practically of scattering the Word of God and investing into people's lives. It would be unwise to stop giving to God and the Kingdom of God. It may go against our human nature to scatter what we have, but we cannot afford not to give.

8. *'Honour the LORD with your substance, and with the first fruits of all your increase so your barns will be filled with plenty, and your presses will burst out with new wine.'*[16] When you honour someone you are showing respect and being loyal and faithful. God will always bless those who are loyal to him.

9. *'While the earth remains, seedtime and harvest, cold and heat, summer and winter, and day and night will not cease.'*[17] There is always a time to sow and harvest. God cannot lie, and if he promises a harvest, it surely has to follow the sowing part. This includes spiritual and natural sowing rewards.

10. Remember Melchizedek, King of Salem, priest of the Most High God, King of righteousness, King of peace. *'Now consider how great this man was, to whom even the patriarch Abraham gave a tenth of the spoil.'*[18] Tithing was introduced by Abraham. It is a way to be consistently faithful, and provide a means of income for the Kingdom of God. This book is not a tithing book, and if you feel you need further understanding on this subject, you may wish to consider the book by Michael Torres, *The Rediscovery of the Warfare Tithe.*

Some people say that as we are saved by grace, we do not need to tithe as the Old Testament saints did under the Law. However, the book of Hebrews shows and confirms that tithing is an act of worship seen by the example of Abraham and Levi to Melchizedek.

I understand 90 per cent of the UK population does not use their commercial investment entitlement in the stock exchange before they get taxed (currently up to £10,000). Do we have the same problem today in a spiritual sense in the church of the living God? If we do not make wise investments, either spiritually as explained in the above list and be rich towards God, or monetary as we see the commercial opportunities arise, then we are not using our entitlement to the maximum and we may be in lack when we do not need to be.

Our lack can sometimes be apportioned to the fact that we have neglected sound advice. Some opportunities repeat frequently: daily, weekly, monthly and annually; whereas some opportunities can be lost, they are for a moment in time

This was the case for the children of Israel and partly the reason why they ended up in Egypt and Babylon. Israel's love of money and not honouring God's Word was their downfall and lost opportunity. God had specifically provided guidance on how to maintain the land and crops: rest the land every seventh year. For us today, a practical example can be drawn from the ever increasing property market that has ballooned because of the growth in buy-to-let properties. I am not saying buy-to-let is wrong; however we should balance our investments wisely, always keeping our duty to God.

Let's now understand a little deeper why Israel ended up in Egypt and Babylon. Israel ended up in affliction and sojourning for 430 years.[19] The Israelites' captivity was brought about because of greed, the love of money, and by not honouring the Word of God to rest the land every seven years. When things go wrong, sometimes we are quick to blame the devil or the latest Pharaohs, but usually the fault lies with us. God had provided the Israelites with a principle of how to look after the land. This is very similar to the UK fascination with escalating property prices and the need to keep moving to a bigger and more profitable property. God had provided some sound advice regarding the Sabbath years.[20] The Israelites were told to rest the land every seventh year, but they ignored the advice and kept over-farming. What did this lead to? Seventy years of captivity under Babylonian rule all because they did not honour God's Word of resting the land.[21]

Macedonian church

The Macedonian church was the poorest church region in modern church history but they received God's abounding grace due to their faith.[22] As mentioned earlier, it was the Macedonian church's generosity that inspired me to write this book. For the purpose of this book, our focus is on good choices.[23]

In 2 Corinthians 8 Paul writes his second instruction to the church in Corinth, the richest and largest region in Greece. History shows that Corinth was richer and bigger than even Athens, the capital of Greece. Paul also makes reference to the poorest region of churches in Macedonia at a time when Macedonia was in deep poverty.

For me the most amazing part of this story is that the Macedonian churches were the poorest group of churches in Greece, but it was this same poverty-stricken region that made the investment to support Paul and Titus. It was Titus that went on to save Corinth. It was Paul's and Titus' faith that relied on the church's funding for their activities and it was the Macedonian region that trusted God.

Titus did minister in Macedonia, but he mainly carried out this work in Corinth. Titus was funded by the poor to help the richer churches. Often we give from our wealthy positions, but here we read and learn about ridiculous faith and gospel generosity. The churches in Corinth were in so much disorder, from immature spiritual understanding to sexual immorality. They were out of control, even eating their lunch during the breaking of bread service. Corinth, in their wealth, had no respect for the Word of God. It was Titus who was hands-on, who implemented church order face-to-face with this out-of-control behaviour. It is much easier to teach face-to-face and talk than send letters. In Whitehall we have people debating; in Afghanistan we have people implementing. There is a difference when you are hands-on. A good investment is to either provide for a person that needs your help regardless of your financial position, or be the implementer. (See Chapter 6 'Implementing the Plan'.)

Pure gospel is to think of others, to provide and sacrifice something (e.g. time, money, help or service to others). What is the best choice and investment that anyone can make to actively support others in need? Jesus making himself poor to provide his life as the ultimate sacrifice for mankind is the ultimate investment: *'For you know the grace of our Lord Jesus Christ, that though He was rich, yet for your sakes He became poor, that through His poverty you might be rich.'*[24] This was the solid foundation that the Macedonians stood by. Nobody told them to give, they just spontaneously responded to the need to support the gospel of Christ by funding and sending Titus. The Macedonians lack of wealth or well-being was not mentioned; their focus was to give regardless of their own situation.

In contrast, the story of the Good Samaritan is where the priestly body of the day got it totally wrong. The priests looked at the man who was half dead and in great need and crossed the road and looked on. The Samaritan made the right basic choices. This unnamed Samaritan naturally helped nurse the man's wounds, and provided a transport system to safety to help him to recovery. He invested from his own pocket by paying the innkeeper to look after the injured man until he recovered. The gospel always helps us to focus on the right things in life, to act brilliantly on Christian basics.

The Good Samaritan had enough funds to pay the innkeeper to provide the nursing recovery time, shelter and refreshments until the wounded man got better. Many people focus on the Samaritan's actions to help, but miss the point about being able to finance the help required. This good man had made some good choices behind the scenes so that, when the need arose, he was able to instantly help the person in need.

Sometimes credit is given to England for spreading the Good News, due to the Bible being translated from Latin into English and the ministering of the Holy Spirit at the beginning of the nineteenth century. If we take a step back in time and map the history, we will find that the Macedonians made the right choices and provided the investment. I would consider the credit should go to the group of churches in Macedonia as this was the first stronghold of Christianity in Europe. The investment that the Macedonians made in their poverty led to the Word of God reaching Africa, America, the Caribbean, India and the Far East – in effect worldwide. That Word eventually reached the United Kingdom and the rest of the history is well documented from this point. I just want us to remember where the seed was planted and how making good choices can exceed our imaginations, which will spread and last from generation to generation.

Chapter 8 of 2 Corinthians definitely makes me think where I should be making my next spiritual investment. If I do something now for God, it will be expedited to another generation from a chain of events that might not be recognised at the time of planting that spiritual or practical seed.

Let's look at evangelism for a moment.

There is plenty of harvest (opportunity), however there are very few effective labourers who are willing to stick the sickle in[25] (operate within the opportunity) to help others find Christ. We have the liberty to evangelise everywhere. Whoever invests their time and effort in this spiritual occupation of evangelism will receive great rewards in heaven. The angels rejoice over one sinner who repents.[26] On earth you will see the hearts of men and women transformed.

As people change for the better and bring their lives into order with Jesus, growth will be experienced in the church from everyone involved. Issues may arise from the 'old man'[27] the carnal side of the new creature in Christ.[28] The church is the support mechanism for the new person in Christ; it is the church members who help to take the bandages off [29] the person who was dead in their sins to make them into a new creature.

Evangelism is the best investment that we can make in the world. When we evangelise, we are giving our free time and spiritual service to help spread the gospel of Jesus Christ.

Successful evangelism is all about praying for lost souls and helping people in need: a soup kitchen or coffee morning or standing in the market talking about the love of Jesus for the world. This will provide the best feeling and fulfilment that you will feel and experience. Be aware, though, you may have to fight against the flesh and feeling ashamed.

Just as you may sow seeds and you see plant life come out of the ground, or go fishing and use different bait to catch fish, when you evangelise for souls, it is the same method utilising practical and spiritual methods of sowing – what you sow, that you will reap.[30]

Endnotes

1. Matthew 27:57
2. Luke 10:25–37
3. Proverbs 23:4
4. Proverbs 3:5
5. Proverbs 11:24
6. 1 Timothy 6:6–11
7. Philippians 4:11–14
8. Luke 16:19–31
9. 2 Corinthians 9:6
10. 2 Corinthians 9:7
11. 2 Corinthians 9:9
12. 2 Corinthians 9:10
13. Luke 6:38
14. Proverbs 23:4
15. Proverbs 11:24
16. Proverbs 3:9–10
17. Genesis 8:22
18. Hebrews 7:1–4
19. Exodus 12:40
20. Leviticus 25

21. 2 Chronicles 36:19–21
22. 2 Corinthians 8 & 9
23. 2 Corinthians 8:1–7
24. 2 Corinthians 8:9
25. Mark 4:29
26. Luke 15:10
27. Romans 6:6
28. 2 Corinthians 5:17
29. John 11:44
30. Galatians 6:7

4
The Spirit of a Giving Church

Have you ever wondered what propels someone to give and another person not to give?

When I observe people, especially families, I notice how some families greet each other with a kiss and a hug, and others might just nod or shake hands. I have concluded this tends to come down to their upbringing and what they have learnt from their parents or guardians. This principle of learning from others may be the link to the generosity shown by some individuals. From an early age they may have been taught to share toys, their meals, offer some of their pocket money to charity or church offerings, for example. So when they have grown up with this principle, it becomes part of their DNA. Right from an early stage, they are now familiar with the principle of giving and sharing and caring for others.

The spirit of a giving church, therefore, needs to come from the pastor down to the members. So when people visit or become members of a church community, they experience and are part of that gift of love of giving to others from the heart. It becomes part of their DNA to help out at the soup kitchen, coffee morning and so forth. It is a constant chain of events that builds into the personality of a person and the heart of the church.

Jesus refers to an example of giving when he was sitting near the treasury at the temple. Jesus observed the rich were providing a gift from their abundance to the treasury. We are not told all the details, but I guess there must have been a disapproving way of how the rich were presenting their gifts. Perhaps the amount was announced or presented in such a way that everyone could see or know. Assuming the gift could not be hidden, it would have been easier to notice the individuals providing large gifts, allowing human nature to take its course.

God always has a way of making an example of human nature and bringing out the faith and grace of the Spirit of God. What made the widow give away her life's savings?[1] The widow did not have a spouse to provide for her, a nest egg or pension system to rely on. What was her concern, or her need? It has to be that this widow had complete faith and trust in God to provide for her. In order to have this type of faith and understanding of God, this widow needed to be connected to him from the scriptures of the Old Testament.

What scriptures and examples would this widow draw on from the past? Perhaps the following would provide some insights: *'He who has pity on the poor lends to the LORD, and HE will repay what he has given.'*[2]

God's words are true, he cannot lie, so if he says he will provide for us when we provide for others in need, this act of gratitude from us can now open up a whole new spiritual blessing. God has the ability to bless individuals and church regions which are beyond their means to be blessed, whereby God can pour out his favour and his blessing upon us that give, straight from his window in heaven. God's window may well be a metaphor, but the blessings are real. When I think of God's window, I am not thinking of a little slit that you might see in a castle, or the windows in my house; I think that God's windows are much, much bigger than that.

David wrote down in his old age one of his psalms to say that he had always been blessed during all the years he had lived on the planet: *'I have been young, and now am old; yet I have not seen the righteous forsaken, nor their offspring begging bread.'*[3]

How comforting to know that God will look after us from all walks of life and ages to come. It might not be in a manner that we are expecting, but God will never let his people down. One of the laws of the harvest that we find in the book of Leviticus is designed to help those that have not: *'When you reap the harvest of your land, you shall not reap your field up to the edge, nor shall you gather any gleaning of your harvest. You shall leave them to the poor and to the foreigner: I am the LORD your God.'*[4]

From this principle, Ruth was able to glean the corn left in the corner of the field that belonged to Boaz, to provide for herself and Naomi.[5]

Another example of God's provision can be taken from the story of the widow of Zarephath, who we will look at in greater detail.[6] Elijah the Tishbite declared a drought to demonstrate to Ahab that God is omnipotent. God is in control of the weather systems as well as reigning on the just and unjust. Following the ravens feeding Elijah bread and meat at the brook of Cherith, Zarephath is chosen to sustain Elijah. When the brook dried up, God sent another word to Elijah to go into Sidon. As Elijah approached the gate of the city he saw the widow and her son as they were gathering sticks. The whole of the Middle East, if not the world, was suffering from Elijah's faithful word, not just the Jordan area.

'*I have commanded a widow there to provide for you.*' [7] God will always keep you going. Now for faith to work, you need the chain of trust . . . all parties need to be connected to one another. Elijah was sent to a woman who had no man providing for her at a time of just under three years into the story of praying for no rain and the famine was raging.

Sometimes God will send you to a place that does not look right. Elijah sees a woman who is starving to death (a kind of a church), with a child who is skin and bone. The widow sees Elijah who is well nourished because he has been fed by the ravens. The chain of trust in God is required in all three parties: God with the prophet and the widow and vice versa back to God. Elijah sees a woman and a son about to use up their last handful of meal and oil. But the widow is commanded to sustain Elijah even though she and her son are about to die. If the chain of trust breaks then no miracles for that day will happen. The game changer is the chain of trust not to be broken.

Elijah requested a small cup of water and, as the widow woman went to fetch the water, Elijah then requested a morsel of bread. This is an act of faith being questioned. The widow then informed the man of God of her plight, that they were about to have their last meal wrapped around the two sticks, and die, such was the small quantity of flour and oil. Sometimes in life God will ask us to choose from fleshly things and spiritual things. This takes great faith. God's preference is for man to experience the risk of faith and life, rather than the eating and dying.

Compare this story with Jacob and Esau, when Esau sold his

birth right for a bowl of red lentils. We should never sell our birth right. Nor should we allow our stomachs to rule our decisions.

The widow woman in the book of Kings honoured God's instruction at all times, even though she was on the brink of death. This final act of faith enabled Elijah to bless the widow and her son by providing flour and oil until the rain was sent. What I like about this story is that it was not just the widow and the son who benefited from the blessing; it was her whole household. Reading between the lines, I believe the widow found she had many relations and friends who made their way to her house to be part of her household and the blessing. Just like the church, if we put good food on the table the people will find their way. The additional benefit of this act of trust and faith by the widow is revealed later on in the story when her son became ill and died. Having complete faith in the man of God she went to Elijah who revived her son back to life.

Helping the church body to flourish

Fundamentally, the church body is made up of all sorts of different groups, organisations and independent churches. Wherever you find yourself, there will be a group for you. If not, then there may be an opportunity to start something as long as God is directing you that way. Wherever you find yourself, and as long as you are part of that entity, I feel it is important to be involved as much as you can, and give back to your local community.

Moses in the book of Numbers[8] and Jesus' disciples in the book of Matthew[9] both asked the same question: *'How do we feed so many people in the wilderness?'*

In Moses' case, the children of Israel walked repeatedly in

circles during the early years of their forty years in the wilderness; they were fed up with the manna – bread from heaven – which the Israelites needed to collect each day to grind to make flour for bread. They wanted meat, so they complained bitterly. This displeased God, for they did not understand that God was providing them with the best food possible for their well-being.

In the disciples' case, the multitude had been following Jesus for three days and the people had run out of food. The multitude numbered four thousand, and although the people were not complaining, Jesus had compassion on them and did not wish them to go home hungry. Wherever there are people, there will always be a need to feed the sheep.[10] The best way to prepare for this eventuality is to be continually in help mode. You do not need to be a Moses or a Peter to help someone; you just need to be prepared to help someone so the Kingdom of God can flourish.

If our focus is to only receive the Word of God from a TV ministry or popping into our local church and we are not involved in that local church, we may well be missing out on the all-important part of Christianity: to enlist in helping the community. If we are not part of a community church, we may feel something is missing either in our life or the part of the church body we attend. When our focus is on helping people we will be getting the best out of the ministry because each good investment we make in Christ will result in the best return you can imagine.[11]

The gift of giving by the Macedonians was by God's grace
In Paul's description of the zeal of Titus to the churches in

Corinthians and how Titus inspired the Macedonians to give to the Corinthians, Paul identified that it was the grace of God that came upon the Macedonians and then flowed to the Corinthian churches. *'God is able to make all grace abound toward you, so that you, always having enough of everything, may abound to every good work.'*[12]

We know that grace is God's unmerited favour: there is unconditional love regardless of what we have said and done to God. God is always looking for a channel to extend his love and power. The channel of God's grace can be extended to us. Our motive would always need to be pure. While the Macedonians were in deep poverty, they had great joy. There was no collective moaning like Moses suffered from the children of Israel in the wilderness.

The Macedonians received to their confidence, power beyond their ability to give. They had a kind of confidence that was not manufactured by man, but they had confidence in God. *'For the LORD will be your confidence, and will keep your foot from being caught.'*[13]

Upon this God-given confidence, the Macedonians prayed for Paul and Titus to receive a gift. This gift is given of themselves to the needs of the church. At the time, the churches in Corinth thought they were very rich, but had lost their focus on the true riches of God and needed Paul and Titus to be sent to preach and teach the undiluted Word of God.

Paul provides some insight on a true saying and shows how man can let himself or herself down. *'As it is written, "He who gathered much had no excess. And he who gathered little had no lack."'*[14]

Like many who gather much, the Corinthians had nothing left over. It is not always the most obvious channel that will provide the blessing to the kingdom. Following on in the chapter,[15] we see that Paul had great confidence in the underprivileged Macedonians. Paul wrote to the Philippians about confidence: *'I do not speak because I have need, for I have learned in whatever state I am to be content.'*[14]

To have great confidence in this circumstance, Paul is referring to a situation of having confidence and faith against all odds. A good example is the woman of Canaan whose daughter was 'severely possessed by a demon'.[16] The woman is persistent to get the answer she needs. She came to find Jesus and cried unto Jesus in desperation saying, *'Have mercy on me, O Lord, Son of David.'* But there was silence from Jesus, and she chased his disciples for help. The initial response from Jesus was to say nothing. Quite often our first request to God does not get an answer. The woman was so desperate and loud that she did not give up pestering Jesus and his disciples, even though she was being ignored. Her great confidence helped to overcome the rejection of the law (Canaanites were not friends with the Jews). This is one of the key aspects of faith and confidence that we need to have. Just keep going until you hear from God.

The disciples wanted Jesus to *'send her away'* and have nothing to do with her, but Jesus answers his disciples and says, *'I was sent only to the lost sheep of the house of Israel.'* Then, she came to him and worshipped him saying desperately, *'Lord, help me.'*

Jesus answers the third time and speaks to her directly after she worships him and requests help. *'It is not fair to take the children's bread and to throw it to dogs.'* This is a harsh response from Jesus;

most people at this point may have walked away feeling rejected and missed out on their blessing of the miracle.

However, the woman with no name does not give up on her request for help: *'She said, "Yes, Lord, yet even dogs eat the crumbs that fall from their masters' table."'* When Jesus hears the woman reply in humility and confidence in her faith in Jesus, that just one crumb from the table would help to heal her daughter, Jesus answers again directly to the woman the fourth time: *'Then Jesus answered her, "O woman, great is your faith. Let it be done for you as you desire." And her daughter was healed instantly.'* Notice it took four answers from Jesus before the woman received the answer she was looking for. This persistent journey by this woman from Canaan of a conversation, prayer or request to Jesus, demonstrated her great faith in him which was visible to everyone. Sometimes our requests to Jesus are far too quiet, and perhaps we give up too soon on Jesus. This example encourages us to keep on believing, not to give up on our miracle that we need to happen, or keep going until our dreams materialise. Due to this woman's great faith, she witnessed and experienced a miracle instantly.

Back to Paul. Paul identifies that when we sow, it is really down to a matter of our faith. The word says, *'He who sows sparingly . . .'*[17] When we have faith, giving is not an issue for us, either before the giving or after. If we hold back our faith or our trust in God, then the return on our investments will be small as we have only partly given. The scripture says 'sparingly'. The best thing here is to just give and God will provide for our needs.

How to get the spirit of a giving church

I have noticed as recession and prosperity travels the world, a spirit of self-centredness increases, as does obesity and medical conditions. In some parts of the world we have adults and children dying of malnutrition, they are homeless and penniless; yet there is a growth in millionaires and the purchase of extravagant homes. What a dichotomy! From my personal experience, I have seen a change in my life when I think of others and act upon it, whether in this country or abroad. This is a spiritual law that is recognised in heaven.

When we look at the region of the churches of Macedonia, they thought of others who were actually financially better off, but spiritually worse off. This was a very different and unusual circumstance because the money was found in the poorest region of Macedonia to provide the teacher, Titus, to restore and correct the church in Corinth, the wealthiest church in Europe. When the churches in Corinth accepted the messages from Titus, the wealth in Corinth was utilised in Europe for the Kingdom of God and for the Word of God to spread. England is very often acknowledged for spreading the gospel around the world, but for me this would have never happened if the Macedonians had not sent the offering to Titus. Through Titus' preaching and teaching he set the Corinthians free, breaking them from their spiritual immaturity.

To me this is an example of how God works: the supernatural God providing the answer by using something that man would not use. Only God would ask a widow who is suffering, starving and close to death from famine, to provide her last meal for the man of God.

Regardless of your situation, God can do anything for you to receive the word that you need to release you from your circumstance.

As I close this chapter, full credit should to go to the churches in Macedonia as they implemented the most faithful offering in early church history. I do not think they stuck to a 10 per cent tithe offering but, rather, they gave from their heart and gave much more. I am not sure if you may be wrestling with your own conscience and asking yourself questions about what you can do to help others. The best thing to do is not to think too long, but to just start helping your local community and church. Find out what they need and start volunteering. In church we can be willing to open up the doors and provide prayer and time to listen to people's needs. We can invest our time, pass on our skills, knowledge and finance and do this with a willing heart.

We can look for more pressing needs and dream up ways of being able to give back to our local community and church.

Endnotes

1. Mark 12:41–44
2. Proverbs 19:17
3. Psalm 37:25
4. Leviticus 23:22
5. Ruth 2:2
6. 1 Kings 17
7. 1 Kings 17:9
8. Numbers 11:13
9. Matthew 15:33
10. John 21:15–17
11. Matthew 10:40–42
12. 2 Corinthians 9:8
13. Proverbs 3:26

14. 2 Corinthians 8:15
15. 2 Corinthians 8:22
16. Matthew 15:21–28
17. 2 Corinthians 9:6

5
God's Ways Are Not Our Ways

This story of the Macedonian churches really grips me and highlights more than ever that God's ways are not our ways. My faith, and yours too, is built up if we accept the unexplainable situations that arise and testify of his marvellous light and grace that is bestowed upon us. All too often we use our carnal ways, utilising man-made strategies to lead when, if we would take the example of Paul and Titus and be led by the Spirit of God, the unexplainable will provide the unexpected result.

To be led by the Spirit, we need to allow God to lead us by the Spirit. We need to have a connection and relationship in devoted prayer with him and move away from any issues that might be distracting us, such as worry or sinful thoughts or deeds. It is essential that we hear his quiet, calm voice in the storm. If our lives are full of activities 24/7, and we do not make regular time to pray, we will be running on our own steam, drinking energy drinks and relying on soundbites and motivational quotes on Facebook to try and compensate for real devotion with Jesus. We must not kid ourselves or believe that we have heard from God if we do not have time to pray one-to-one with him or, within groups, to seek his face. The length of prayer is not so much the issue, although Jesus requested his disciples to pray for an hour with him. The content and the belief in the actual prayer requests is key. God needs to be able to hear your prayer from heaven. Our pride of life can stop our words from our mouth reaching him. We do not need to shout for him to hear us; we just need to be humble to get results, so we do not pray amiss. It is good to have a quiet time following our prayer to allow God to speak into our heart. There is nothing wrong in double checking to make sure you heard God speak to you correctly.

'If My people, who are called by My name, will humble themselves and pray, and seek My face and turn from their wicked ways, then I will hear from heaven, and will forgive their sin and will heal their land.'[1]

'If' is the stipulation, the condition. We need to decide to select this good choice to enable our prayers to be answered. Our 'old man' carnal ways may not want to do this God's way, however God has promised to answer our prayers if we follow this pattern and prayer model. There are many other prayer models in the Scriptures that you can use to help you hear from God. Personally, I buy books about prayer to help me develop and be effective in my prayer life. I then tend to follow the book and try out the different methods that may suit me or challenge me to increase my intensity in my prayer life.[2]

Focus on Titus

So who was Titus? Was he was a well-known preacher with a big reputation, with a history of demonstrating miracles or leading large groups of people from sin and bringing them to Christ? Well, Titus is not mentioned in the book of Acts and is only mentioned in the books of Galatians and Corinthians. I could not find any evidence of Titus demonstrating any leadership skills at the time of being sent to the church in Corinth.

Titus was a convert of Paul's preaching; he was just one of the students that helped Paul to deliver the word. Titus, like Timothy, was a young person growing up in the Lord, possibly with no past experience of ministry, doing the job that he was sent to do. Perhaps he was just believing, trusting, obedient and loyal to Jesus and Paul. If we were faced with a similar situation today, we would have looked for a more experienced preacher, with a reputation of preaching to tens of thousands; someone with a pedigree and credentials of past crusades and a list of miracles behind their name. This was not the case for Titus. God sent Titus via Paul as he was humble.

The prophet Isaiah wrote (to help us understand how God works) that it is not by normal logical human understanding that we decipher God's works. God can use anyone: a stubborn individual like Jonah or humble pliable servant like Titus. *'For My thoughts are not your thoughts, nor are your ways My ways, says the Lord. For as the heavens are higher than the earth, so are My ways higher than your ways, and My thoughts than your thoughts.'*[3]

Jeremiah, too, provided insights and words of comfort on how God thinks at a time when Jerusalem had fallen and judgement was upon Israel. Judah had backslidden from God, leading to many Jews residing in Egypt as refugees. Some would think that God does not love his people, but again, in times of war and loss of homes and land, God's ways are not our ways. God has a great plan for us. *'For I know the plans that I have for you, says the Lord, plans for peace and not for evil, to give you a future and a hope.'*[4]

Even in a time of sickness, flood, famine, war, incarceration and disaster, God has a plan of hope for us; an escape route of peace. God is not evil – he is a God of love. The crimes of war and destruction arrive from the devil not God. If we find ourselves in times of terror, then we do need to pray ourselves out of that situation. Judah had backslidden and forgot to pray to God for protection. Prayer makes the difference. Through Jeremiah, God gave Judah forty years to repent. God is longsuffering to us; he would not want any of us to perish without him.

In Chapter 2 we looked at David, who was left out of the original invite to witness the prophet Samuel anointing one of the sons of Jesse. David was the youngest and only a lad, not like his eldest brother Eliab. But God chose to use David rather than his seven older brothers. God looks at our heart and not our height or our job title or our gender. God is not a respecter of persons; his ways are not our ways.

The next section in the book swiftly looks at many well-known characters in the Bible who were selected to serve him, or became a witness without the spiritual credentials that one would expect. To repeat myself, God's ways are not our ways, and we cannot second guess what God will do for his people.

Here are a few examples demonstrating that God's ways are not our ways:

Right from creation God used faith to frame the world. He used the Word to create the heavens, the earth and the universe. He just spoke things through faith into existence. God spoke *'let there be light'* and there was. God uses invisible things to keep the stars and planets in position. God only knows what holds the planets in place; scientists still do not understand creation, but we believe and know he used his faith.

God used the dust of the earth to create Adam, the first man, and into this image he breathed life, and man lived. No one person understands the whole of the human body, but we have different doctors who specialise in specific areas. From:

Audiologists who look after hearing,

Allergists who treat allergies,

Anaesthesiologists who focus on pain,

Cardiologists who understand issues with the heart,

Dentists who look after our teeth,

Dermatologists who take care of the skin,

Endocrinologists who understand the glands in the body,

Epidemiologists who search for diseases,

Gynaecologists who specialise in the female reproductive organs,

Immunologists who look into the immune system,

Medical Geneticists who treat genetic disorders,

Microbiologists who look into infectious bacteria and viruses that attack the body,

Neurologists who look into the brain,

Obstetricians who focus on child birth,

Oncologists who look into the prevention of cancer,

Orthopaedic surgeons who understand the skeletal system,

ENT specialists who look into the ear, nose and throat,

Paediatricians who work on infants and children,

Physiologists who understand the state of the human body including the emotions,

Podiatrists who understand the feet and ankles,

Psychiatrists who study behaviour,
Radiologists who detect physiological ailments by x-rays,
Rheumatologists who treat conditions that affect the joints,
Surgeons of all different kinds and
Urologists who understand the urinary system.[5]

Yet Jesus understands all the needs of the person and can fix, heal and even raise the dead. All we can do is ask for the Master Physician to intercede for us.

After the creation of Adam, God introduces Eve. God puts Adam to sleep and uses Adam's rib to create Eve. Hopefully by now you are getting the picture that God is marvellous in what he can do for us.

God blessed Isaac when Isaac sowed in faith, at a time when the land had suffered two great famines one after another. Today we would call that a double-dip recession, however the land produced a hundredfold return, at a time when the land was like a desert.

God blessed Job with five more children following his great loss of family and commercial ruin. Job received a double portion blessing when he reflected on his character and got rid of his anger (the Leviathan who was troubling him with his mood swings).

Abraham and Sarah waited 25 years for their promised son, Isaac, who came to them when they were a hundred years old. When Sarah died, about 20 years later, Abraham remarried and had many more children. Note: a miracle is not just for one day; when God blesses you, you're blessed.

God used stuttering Moses to withstand the mighty Pharaoh

and lead his people out of a foreign land.

God uses a starving widow of Zarephath who, under the Jewish law, was seen as a no-good Gentile, to feed his prophet Elijah. This suffering woman was about to have her last meal of flour and oil with her son, but was requested to use the ingredients to make cake for the prophet Elijah. When she follows the instructions in faith and in obedience to God's Word, she and her son are blessed. The flour and oil remained constant until the rain fell. This might sound ridiculous or bizarre in our natural carnal state of mind, but God works differently to how we expect.

God used the praise of his people to bring down the walls of Jericho without the need for earthquakes, explosives, battering rams or any other type of assistance – just the praise of the Israel nation.

God uses Jephthah, the son of a harlot, who was chased out of the family home by his step brothers when they discovered his past, to lead Israel and defeat the Ammonites. Interestingly, the same brothers who chased him and led him to his homeless state were instrumental in assisting Jephthah defeat the Ammonites.[6]

God used a donkey to speak to Balaam, to stop Balaam in his tracks on his way to see Balak, so that Balaam would not be slain by an invisible angel of the Lord.[7]

God used the stubborn and reluctant Israeli preacher, Jonah, to save the great Babylon city of Nineveh from destruction by calling a three-day fast.[8]

God used David, when he was only a lad, to slay Goliath with one of the five stones he took from the stream. The Philistine giant Goliath, standing six feet plus in all his armour and splendour with his sword in hand, asked for a man to fight, but lost to a boy with a sling shot.[9] What an encouraging story we all love to hear again and again. Even in the news today when someone might be described as small, insignificant, unknown, and wins in the court room against a big multinational, they always refer to the 'David and Goliath' battle, particularly if the small company wins a litigation battle.

The incarnation of Jesus, meaning God's union with man, was made flesh and then crucified on the cross, to save the world from their sins. Jesus' blood is used and referred to as taking away the sins of the world, as there is no remission without the shedding of the blood.

This is the way that God decided to save man, and on the third day Jesus was raised from the dead identifying that only God himself could perform such an act of love, power and restoration.

Jesus took a boy's lunch of five loaves and two fish to feed 5000 people (although there were more, as the women and children weren't included in the count), and still had twelve baskets of breadcrumbs remaining for the disciples to collect.

In every instance above, God uses faith sometimes as small as the mustard seed to implement his will and his blessings.

We must use faith in every instance to thrive

We are all born with *'the measure of faith'*[10] which God has granted to us. It is how we come to empower our faith towards God that will make the difference in our lives. We are all blessed with gifts of some sort; we are all born with faith to apply to our lives regardless of whether we believe in God or not. We have to apply faith to our lives to find God and our purpose in this Christian walk. We have free access by faith in Jesus who provided liberation and the keys to the Kingdom of God. Faith abides with hope and love.

There is a whole chapter in Hebrews dedicated to faithful characters whereby they came by faith or went through faith to achieve God's purpose. God is faithful; faith is increased when we hear the Word of God. We walk by faith and not by sight. We are saved by faith. Faith is the means by which man accepts and receives God's saving grace, thus faith is the channel through which God's grace comes to man. *'Without faith it is impossible to please God.'*[11]

We are justified by faith; we live by faith. We add virtue to our faith by God's grace. People are healed by faith, and people are delivered by faith. Faith is a fruit and a gift of faith. We can pray in faith; one can demonstrate great faith as faith is not limited by geography. Jesus marvelled at the centurion's great faith; faith is part of our armour, the shield of faith. *'Jesus [is] the author and finisher of our faith.'*[12] We can have a test of faith, like Job. The brother of Jesus, James, dedicates a book about faith, highlighting that faith without works is dead.[13]

Faith is defined as *'the substance of things hoped for, the evidence of things not seen'*.[14] Faith is a strong, mighty, powerful force in the spirit world. Faith deals with the invisible spirit substance used to create things desired. God used his faith to create the world. Faith is released by speaking. When Jesus cursed the fig tree, the tree dried up from the roots.[15] When we speak in faith, we have to speak to the root cause not just the surface level.

The Feast of Trumpets was for everyone to celebrate with the king. Trumpets are used for royal occasions and also in times of battle. Before the actual victory is realised the trumpets are blown in faith to celebrate the victory ahead. Here are some encouraging examples of unique examples of faith.

- Noah saved his family in the ark from the flood – by faith Noah preached 120 years. By God's grace eight souls were saved.
- Moses, by faith, led Israel out of Egypt by participating in the Passover Lamb and crossing the Red Sea to the Promised Land. By God's covering and protection they survived and escaped.
- Israel survived and escaped Assyrian and Babylonian rule as God remembered his covenant promise with Abraham.
- Daniel in the lion's den escaped by his unwavering, untouchable faith in God.
- The three Hebrew boys were seen dancing in the fire with a fourth person who looked like the son of man (Jesus). By their praise and great faith in God they escaped Nebuchadnezzar's plan of destruction.
- Job escaped the Leviathan test by his faithful persistent belief in his God. Job escaped the attack of the devil and his faith was rewarded with double for his trouble.
- Rahab and her family escaped destruction by faith.
- David escaped the madness of Saul by his faith in God.
- The thief on the cross was redeemed by his recognition and faith in Jesus. In his last breath, the thief was saved. What a remarkable great escape.

The book of Proverbs gives an insight on how to think with faith regarding a purpose driven attitude to life.[16]

In the natural, faith works. In the 2004 Olympics the British cyclist Chris Hoy won a gold medal in Athens. His father said, when interviewed after the race, that his son had focused on the games since the age of thirteen. The young boy had written in his diary that in August 2004 he would win a gold medal for cycling. Words are powerful; they are like containers that carry faithful requests to their destination. Negative words can be stopped in their tracks as negative words will only hinder or stop success. The word 'can't' sends shockwaves of panic through the communication system within a human, and can prevent us from moving forward.

Job

Let's take a closer look at Job to see what we can learn about how he worshipped and provided thanksgiving to God whilst he was being tested on all fronts.

All Bible scholars agree that the book of Job is the oldest book in the Bible. It was actually written before Genesis, probably around 4500–4000 BC. The book of Job is also the oldest book in the world (set in the land of Uz in the east, not Israel), possibly around Abraham's time, before Moses – there are no references to the Red Sea in the book of Job. From my research and observations, it is fair to say that the first two books ever written are Job and then the Torah which covers the first five books of the Bible (written by Moses). Job relates to God as the Almighty God, Jehovah Shaddai.

The book of Job focuses on two loving fathers: our heavenly Father, who is the everlasting Father, the only wise God, the only living God; and Job. Both loving fathers had the same enemy: the fallen angel, Satan. In the first chapter of the book of Job, there was a conversation between God and the devil and, whatever was said, our heavenly Father did not doubt for one minute that Job would fail the challenge. There was no plan B for God. In God's mind the first human father that was ever written about was always going to be triumphant. Job was oblivious to what was in front of him.

'*You do not know what calamity may happen on the earth.*'[17] This is why we keep going and give a portion to seven and also to eight. As leaders, parents, father or mother, we should not be seen as sitting back, resting. We need to be moving forward as leaders for people to look up to as examples.

As fathers we need to keep demonstrating that we keep on working at what we have been blessed with. Solomon was saying we should have more than one avenue to bless God, have more than one income stream; if one gets cut off or blocked, then you have more than one income coming in. Remember, Isaac kept on digging wells until the enemy of despair left him alone.

Job prayed and loved his children, he was perfect and upright, and one that feared God and eschewed evil. He was very prosperous and, as his children feasted, he gave thanks and provided burnt offerings to God. Job did not provide the ten offerings for his children under Mosaic Law, or under duty or due to any Melchizedek encounter like Abraham. Job provided the offerings to God because he loved God.

Job was a loving and giving person, yet something dreadful was about to happen to him. He was about to have his world turned upside down and taken from him. With no warning, Job lost all ten children (seven sons and three daughters) and all of his wealth – all in one day. On the same day that he had worshipped God and given burnt offerings to God for his children.

When all of God's blessings had been taken away from him, he had the integrity and patience to still worship and he prayed to God. Job still stood by his wife even when she mocked him: *'His wife said to him, "Are you still maintaining your integrity? Curse God and die."'*[18] Even his wife questioned his integrity.

As leaders and as fathers or mothers we will feel isolated, our faith will be tested, our finances stretched and tested, our marriage tested, friendships tested; sometimes we will be grieving, too. Sometimes the only thing we have is our integrity to keep on praying to God until something happens.

But if you hit rock bottom and you are still able to love God, then the only way is up. Job still ended up as a blessed man. He was blessed again with another ten children with the same wife. Job is a respected father. Everything you need to know about leadership, being a man with integrity, being a father, spiritual prosperity and patience is all in the book of Job.

Endnotes

1. 2 Chronicles 7:14
2. Ruth Fowke, *Personality and Prayer*, (CWR, 2008)
3. Isaiah 55:8–9
4. Jeremiah 29:11
5. https://blog.udemy.com/different-types-of-doctors/
6. Judges 10:6 –12:7
7. Numbers 22:29
8. Jonah 3
9. 1 Samuel 17
10. Romans 12:3
11. Hebrews 11:6
12. Hebrews 12:2

13. James 2:14–26
14. Hebrews 11:1
15. Mark 11:12–14
16. Proverbs 23:7
17. Ecclesiastes 11:2
18. Job 2:9

6
Implementing the Plan

To set a backdrop for this chapter, I recommend reading Genesis 6:14–22 regarding God providing the instructions to Noah to build the ark, and Matthew 9:37–38, 10:1–15 where Jesus is asking for labourers and then sends his disciples out to preach to the lost; to be evangelists. Both examples provide plans full of statements, instructions, outlines and guidance, but not too many details. Therefore we do need to be able to pray to God for his guidance, as there is space within Jesus' requests to be able to add our spiritual and practical innovations to save the lost.

It is often said that if you have no plan, then you plan to fail, and seven days without praying makes one weak. Prayer is one of those pillars that we need to build into our spiritual house when we are involved in God's plan.

Solomon provided guidance about having a plan in that he focuses on the vision. He wrote *'Where there is no vision, the people perish; but happy is he who keeps the teaching.'*[1]

The type of vision that Solomon was talking about was to prepare and look forward to the future to enable the people that you are serving. Spiritually speaking, only God can guide you in planning for the future. In this chapter I will use the Scriptures as a guide and weave in any practical methods that I can to help you seek his face to help you plan for the future.

What is a plan?

A plan can be a diagram, a map, a table, a chart, a sketch, an arrangement, even a recipe. It is sometimes the case that the manual or recipe does not work or present the result we expect. I can count the numerous times I have earnestly commenced the build before reading the manual, only to find out I should have read the instructions first! A plan is not the finished article; it is an outline to get you from A to B. To plan something means we need to have time to think things through, to make sure we draft things out, allow for budget reviews, make a jobs to-do list, start date, completion date, order and procure materials, employ human resources, include any training, and so forth.

A plan will help you in your decision making to make wise choices for the future in your life. We need to have a good action plan. There is a difference between having a 'plan' and an 'action plan'. The action plan will always work, whereas the best made plans will fail with no action applied or implemented. We need to find lots of energy and patience when trying to build something for the future. Oftentimes, things take longer and cost more to complete than you might originally plan.

We saw in the last chapter when we looked at Jeremiah, that God knows the plans for each and every one of us.[2] We have to keep going and trust God that his plan for our lives will come to fruition.

Once we have a plan from God

To get a plan from God does not just happen when you want it to. We do need to seek his face, and be prepared to wait and listen for his voice to speak to us.

Sometimes what we want to do is not what God wants us to do. The apostle Paul wanted to go to Asia to preach; the Holy Spirit forbade him to go.[3] During the night, Paul had a night vision, where he saw a man from Macedonia, pleading with him to come.[4] Paul immediately took this as a message to make plans to go to Macedonia.

Once we have a word from God, a plan or a mission, the hardest task of all is to actually start the process. Many of us will have good intentions, but the stumbling block for many is the starting point. To be able to get over the first and second hurdle is the key to success. When the third hurdle comes, you already have a track record.

Another key to success is to do what you do best, 'stick to the knitting'.[5] By all means strengthen your game as an all-round player, but never forget what you do best. This will be your gift, talent or your ability.

So the struggle is getting to first base. Let me use baseball as an analogy. With the baseball bat in your hand, you think, 'I'm going to hit a home run.' But the bowler is not just bowling the ball, he is trying to get you out. The bowler's first ball flies past your eyes. Strike one. You miss the ball.

In preparation for the second ball, you change your footing and concentrate on the bowler. The bowler bowls the second ball; this time with a curve and a spin. You miss it again. Strike two.

Now, in preparation for the third ball, you realise you have to hit it this time or you are out. This time the bowler bowls a slightly wide ball; it passes you by. Your heart flutters, but it's okay, it was a no-ball. You have a reprieve; you have another shot at your last chance. This time it is the last ball. The pressure is on.

Your supporters watch anxiously, half-heartedly smiling. If you miss this one, then the game is over. You check the wind speed, the field, standing position, your grip, your cap – you check everything. The bowler bowls and this time you hit the ball. It shoots straight up in the air, right into the hands of the other side. The ball is dropped. It's a bad hit, but you run for your life. Your heart is beating like crazy, and somehow you slide into first base, just before the ball is thrown to the first base.

The crowd goes crazy and your heart begins to beat fast. The pressure switches from you to the bowler, you are up and running; and you're now in a safe zone at first base. You have to wait for the next batsperson to take their turn before you run to the next stage. This is just like working on a project. Things might not always go your way, and you may have to think on your feet, but just take part and be prepared to run faster than the next person to win.

If we have an action plan, then for sure we will face some obstacles. But as soon as we get the wheels moving, we help to build the momentum – that invisible force to help things move forward – so it is harder for the project to stop. Then you are sure to arrive at your destination and win. For sure, the adversary may be planning to take you out, but the adversary cannot win. However, he can suspend your dream. Our aim is to avoid taking any short-cuts that may lead to birthing an Ishmael! We have to be patient for the momentum to build in whatever we do.

Here are some common indicators and behaviours that may derail your plans or ability to activate your action plan.

1. Being indecisive. This shows a reluctance to commit to decisions. You have a plan but you are not sure. (Remember Lot's wife. The angel held her hand and dragged her down the escape route, but she insisted on looking back.) A lack of faith is the biggest 'derailer' you will face. Do not worry about making some mistakes; it is inevitable. Remember the baseball player: stay focused and just get started.

2. **Difficulty with ambiguity and uncertainty.** We have to deal with fear every day. The Word says 'fear not'. Last month's fear may have been the recession, or Ebola. This month it could be job cuts and next month it could be some other depressing situation. Daily we have to walk by faith and not by sight. 'Trust in the Lord . . . and lean not on thine own understanding.'[1] Trust the Lord that he will not let you down.

3. **Hindering people because of your selfish ways or spiritual jealousy.** Are you aware that your selfishness or spiritual jealousy will hinder the flow in your study group, your prayer group, your choir, your band, your men's group or singles group? It can cause friction in your workplace, your home between friends and family members. It is easy to give someone a hard time if, when you were in training, you received poor treatment or had to struggle to a place of victory. This is not what Jesus would do. If you have been blessed, then bless others with the tools God has bestowed upon you.

4. **Being exclusive and not inclusive.** Each church will have its rules, but when it becomes an exclusive club then we have missed the sweet spot of making everyone feel welcome. Where possible, we need to aim to attract people from different nations into our churches. This helps to protect us

from people saying things about our churches, if we only have one type of person in the church.

5. **Avoid needful conflict.** Conflict with the enemy is a certainty; we cannot accept the worldly attitudes that exist in the world. Noah kept building the ark, regardless of what people said. Conflict with the enemy will make you stronger.

6. **Difficulty building relationships.** For any plan to work, we have to build meaningful relationships. Not just for the current plan, but for the future. Unity helps the anointing to flow. Making people feel involved and getting involved in the plan will help you achieve things much quicker and better than if you try and do everything yourself. When leading a project you have to have a spirit of being able to engage with people who might be different to you and not think like you.

7. **Focus too much on the detail.** God did not tell Noah how many nails to use. I have a feeling that the forest of shittim wood was not on Noah's doorstep. Noah would have to work out how he was going to find the shittim wood and move it from A to B. He had a plan to work to from God, but he needed to work out the details as the building started to take shape. In Matthew we are told to just go, provide neither gold nor silver nor brass. Just take one coat. We are just told the workman is worthy of his meat. With evangelism, we have to work out the where, when and how. God has hired us as labourers; we just need to get stuck into his work, once he has guided us to what he wants us to do.

All we need to do is to implement the Word to our lives.

God is a risk-taker

In all types of plans there is an element of risk. A risk analysis would emphasise the risk afoot, but not necessarily demonstrate that action should not be taken. A good approach would be to avoid exposure to too much risk. Within the banking sector there are aspects of risk, but we still endeavour to deposit our money, despite mistakes occurring within the banking industry. We should not be surprised when this happens; it is inevitable from time-to-time. To implement our plans we need to get used to being responsible for the amount of risk we expose ourselves to and our teams that we work with.

God is a risk-taker in people and spiritual things.

- He gave the most beautiful garden in the world, the Garden of Eden, to Adam to look after.
- He gave Lucifer the honour of leading the choir in heaven.
- Even though God anointed David three times, he still slipped up. In fact all the patriarchs made mistakes.
- Have you considered the conversation between God and Satan regarding Job and his family? God was taking a risk by putting his trust in Job. Judas was handpicked to be one of the twelve disciples but went on to betray Jesus.
- God gave you and me a second chance. In fact he has given us so many chances.

Regardless of the risks, God still continues to sow, because out of the good ground comes life and a return on his investment and trust in us.

The Word is a seed; the Word is an investment; the Word is

a risk to God. I am forever encouraged by the commitment a farmer has towards his crops. Despite the weather reports, a farmer will continue to plant his seed. He takes the risk ahead of knowing what the weather conditions will be. For the farmer holds on to the knowledge of knowing good ground will bring a return, be it one hundred fold, sixty fold or thirty fold. This is his return on investment. The derailers are 'the way side – the birds', 'stony places – scorched', and 'thorns – choked'.[7] The derailers are trying to take away or knock your focus away from the purpose that Jesus set for you.

The farmer knows that there is more good ground than issues, so the farmer takes a risk. Regardless of the weather reports from frosts to storms, droughts and so on. There are 3 or 4 derailers that will not bring in a sustainable return versus the good ground. However, the farmer still goes out to sow because his experience tells him that he will get a return on his investment.

Who has the risk?

In the natural we have choices and we think the risk is with us, when really the risk is with God.

This chapter is for all those with dreams and plans that need to get to first base, past the next challenge or over their next hurdle. God has taken the risk for you. How many times have I made the wrong choice? How many times have you made the wrong choice? What was the outcome? Oftentimes, the results may have been a disaster, a disappointment, or a set-back. I have discovered that on all occasions, the master fixer has been Jesus. He was the one who made the difficult times better, who changed the situation. Yes, it may have been through people or an event, but ultimately God's hand was directing me to the point of resolution. When Peter walked on water the risk was with Jesus. Peter walked calmly on the water towards Jesus until he saw the boisterous winds, at which point Peter's faith diminished and he began to sink. At that point Jesus stretched out his hand to save him. Jesus does want to see us grow in our faith and take risks. For the spiritual ventures he will be there to help us accomplish those things that he has guided us to perform for his kingdom. In the natural he is still watching over us and is there to help guide us. Whatever we need he is there wishing for us to succeed.

It's never too late to implement your dreams and plans

I am still working towards fulfilling my dreams, as I am sure you are too, or maybe you are wishing to find a way to live the dreams that you have had. Despite the downfalls, the diversions, the illusions and even the good times, I am working towards implementing the different plans and dreams, both in the natural and the spiritual.

The same principles apply to both the spiritual and the natural plans and decisions and choices; that is why I have been able to swap between and discuss simultaneously spiritual and natural choices, decisions and plans during this book.

The book of Nehemiah is set in the post-captivity period (after the seventy years of captivity in Babylon; around 539 BC). The book is written to encourage the return of the remnant of Jews back to Jerusalem, to enable the rebuilding of the temple, and the repairing of the walls of the city, including the restoration of the temple worship. The spiritual leaders of this time were the prophets Ezra and Nehemiah.

Nehemiah had the calling from God to rebuild the walls of Jerusalem. He tells King Artaxerxes his calling and Nehemiah starts his work. When the enemy Sanballat, a Moabite of Horonaim who held a command in Samaria, heard that the people were rebuilding the walls of Jerusalem, he got upset and started to say things and mocked the Jews to try and put them off their plans. The spirit of Sanballat is against any kind of revival, or rebuilding, or progress in your prayer life. The spirit of Sanballat will do whatever it can to put up opposition to the work of God. When this happens, we have to declare war in our prayer life. We are not limited by God's grace; we have been given the amour of God to protect ourselves and the plans and dreams that have been given to us. We will experience the same types of oppositions in the natural, within our everyday work life with people in the work environment causing conflicts or criticising our work.

Nehemiah faced six forms of opposition from Sanballat and his troops of destruction:[8]

1. Grief (2:10)
2. Laughter (2:19)
3. Wrath (4:1)
4. Mocking (4:1)
5. Conflict (4:8)
6. Subtlety (6:2–3)

Sanballat and Tobiah in Samaria, the Arabians and the Ammonites and the Ashdodites all heard that the walls of Jerusalem were being rebuilt. When you are making progress, expect someone to criticise you. Sanballat's opposition escalated from morale-damaging mockery to psychological warfare. Very often our battle will be in the mind. The enemy will use emotions to get at you.

Additionally, Nehemiah needed to deal with the people issues of discouragement within his own camp. With all the building there was a lot of debris and rubble. Nobody was cleaning up after themselves and therefore the rubbish started to build up which became a big issue, as the rubbish was cluttering up the rebuilding of the walls.[9]

Nehemiah prayed and reviewed the walls over three nights so as to gather his thoughts and understand the task ahead of him, and allow God to guide him.

Every one of us building something shall face oppositions from all fronts

For those trying to rebuild their life after divorce, they may have opposition as soon as they start the rebuilding process and build their new network of friends around them. In the work environment, when you get promotions, people may say things about you, some of them good and some of them not so nice. If and when we might be implementing change, at work or in church, we will face opposition. We need to learn to be good listeners to determine if there is something that we can learn or anything worthwhile to add to enhance the project.

Whenever someone is getting married, one of the wedding guests will be upset or unhappy with something; we cannot please everyone.

Don't worry if, and when, you're building your spiritual walls of spiritual confidence, that you face the adversary. It is a sign that you're on the right track. Opposition is good for us – it helps to build up our spiritual muscle. We will develop quicker and beyond our original thoughts. It helps us to be more inventive, stronger and even quicker. Usain Bolt needs his Jamaican colleague and friend Yohan Blake to make him go faster and not relax when he is training.

We might not like competition, but it is good for us all. The best thing to do is to embrace the challenges that might be in front of us.

Let's take a look at what happened to Christopher Wren after the Great Fire of London in 1666. Christopher Wren was commissioned to build St Paul's Cathedral. It took him ten years to design. The date of completion of St Paul's is somewhat flexible. The first service was held in the Cathedral Quire is 1697, and the last stone was placed on the lantern in 1710. The pace of construction of the building from 1675 onwards was subject to the availability of resources and design challenges. It is unlikely that an end date was ever properly established. When the building works became delayed, the government of the day halved Wren's pay. He came against all sorts of oppositions for the delays and the costs, but he kept going until it was gloriously completed. St Paul's has survived two world wars, including the 'blitz' when most of the buildings around St Paul's were smashed to pieces. St Paul's Cathedral still stands today as a magnificent place of worship.

Lessons we can learn from the building criteria in Nehemiah

The people that Nehemiah was leading were, in fact, full of

mixed emotions. They would have been worn down from captivity, but yet happy to be back home. They would not have any money, they were suffering from famine, and their beautiful city was in need of drastic repair. The people and the city were not in great shape.

Nehemiah displayed great faith and leadership; his character was full of courage; he demonstrated a 'can do' attitude; he was fearless; he gave the people leadership and direction and a reason to be living; he was enthusiastic and enterprising – a man of prayer and hard work; one who feared God and sought his blessing.

The people had a mind to work, which is a great help to any project that you're working on. The people became proactive in their thoughts. This was not identified until the work was started.

What Nehemiah identified was that when you build something, you naturally start to build up a pile of rubbish, and for you to complete the project *you need to get rid of your rubbish*. In the spiritual you can be working with teams that build up a bad attitude. Sometimes they can pick up a spirit of resentment, un-forgiveness, selfishness and just things that can hinder the building of the project.

The key thing is to de-clutter, in the natural as well as in the spiritual. Whatever your method or purpose we need to enable the team and ourselves to sort things out, strip back, prune, and get rid of the rubbish.

Nine points to help us to de-clutter

1. We need to be focused and thorough, but with balance (we don't want to throw out the baby, with the bathwater). We

may only need to prune rather than chop down.

2. Start straight away. Do not delay. Don't wait for a new year to start something new, when you can start today.

3. If in doubt – chuck it out.

4. Make your mind up.

5. Start straight away with unwanted spirits that may be hovering and surrounding you. *'Get behind me Satan.'*

6. If there are things that keep you awake at night before you pray, de-clutter your mind.

7. Get rid of things that slow you down unnecessarily; or things that delay or distract you. Life is too short; do not let things delay you.

8. Concentrate on one thing that will find you success.

9. From time to time, repeat the process.

Implementing the plan of action

In the book of Genesis, we are acquainted with Noah who implemented the action plan from God when building the ark. Look at these key points:

- Shittim wood is not a soft wood; it is a very durable hardwood which takes twice as much effort to craft.
- The tools used would have been primitive – no German or Japanese engineering here!
- Noah endured 120 years of mockery, yet he completed the plan. There was no practice run. God did not see if the thing would float or that all the joints would hold up. There was no prototype. God used the ark as soon as it was finished.
- By faith Noah implemented the Word of God. I am sure he

would have suffered backache, got splinters in his hands and had frustrations herding the animals and creatures, and perhaps needed to convince his family.

- One small but significant fact is that God waited 120 years for Noah to complete his goal – to save lives. God did not hurry Noah, or give him a time plan to work to. *'Who in times past were disobedient, when God waited patiently in the days of Noah while the ark was being prepared, in which a few, that is, eight souls, were saved through water.'*[10]

Our first steps

How can we match up against the great faith of Noah? The only way we know how is to take the first steps to our first base. An often-used, well-known saying is 'to climb a mountain, we have to take one step at a time'; so it is with any project.

The psalmist encourages us to take these first steps as God is waiting to help us and support us if we fall. *'The steps of a man are made firm by the* LORD; *He delights in his way. Though he falls, he will not be hurled down, for the Lord supports him with His hand.'*[11]

A top practical tip for us all is to avoid letting making money be the main focus and reason for doing something, as people tend to give up if they do not make money straight away. Our focus should be on the gift we have or the dream we want to get right. Finances do need to be considered, but should not be the main focus for utilising our talents.

In the introduction, I mentioned that I started to form new practical and spiritual habits as I started to prepare to write this book. I thought I would share some of these insights with you.

Many years ago I thought of becoming a consultant and working for myself by the age of fifty. About the age of forty-two, in 2007, there was a big change in the company I worked for. The company needed to make some drastic changes and the global roles (including my own) were going to be cut back. I was asked if I wanted to come back and work for them as a consultant for one hundred days per year, which meant I needed to find additional work with other companies.

It was ironic that this is what I really wanted to do later on in life at the age of fifty. This change in the company was a complete surprise to me; it was thrust upon me, much earlier than my original plan. As Solomon would say, *As a man thinks in his heart, so is he.*[12] I took up the challenge and, as all new things, not everything went to the original thoughts and plans. The recession of 2008 was right around the corner, and I soon found out that I needed to find more than one income stream to survive; I needed to diversify. I prayed for some ideas and made up a list of things that I could look at, that would not be a conflict of interest with the consultancy work.

I looked at what I could influence, and came up with some suggestions in the design, packaging and branding of an item that sold well around the world. I bought a shed for the back garden, and started storing some items to sell online. Within a week or two I moved from the shed to the garage, when the main bulk of the stock arrived. I should add here that the main companies that I thought would purchase from me, in my original list of thirty possible contacts, all turned me down. I needed to do a bigger sweep of possible companies and started to call on locations and leave some samples. As soon as I was able to make a few sales, I was then able to say to new clients, I have this product with company X, which built up my confidence when speaking to new opportunities.

My confidence and motivation grew once I had been able to make some sales. I was able to win some business from a high street chain that has implant shops in Harrods and Selfridges. As my main source of income started to become more stable, it became harder for me to physically knock on doors, so I started advertising the details in an industry magazine, and my contact list grew that way. Within twelve months I had moved out of the garage and used space in a warehouse that could store and deliver to customers within forty-eight hours of placing an order anywhere in the UK.

I then looked at what I could do for charities and since 2011 I have been able to invest and provide support to mainly child-focused charities. I have then gone on to volunteer and ran a 10K race for charity. As you can see, one idea leads to another, and when you look back at each stage another step of faith is taken as you expand your faith and abilities. Being constant in helping and giving is just as important as fighting against the attitude of taking things for granted, when you are being blessed.

This secondary income continues to grow each year. With the profit from the secondary income, I have been able to invest in other longer-term projects. None of this would have come about until I took a step of faith and walked into the unknown. Some of the quotes from Warren Buffet in chapter one helped to consolidate my thoughts, along with Ecclesiastes 11 and Psalms 1.

All plans are accomplished by the following characteristics:

- Your goal has to be measurable.
- Agree with yourself and others involved in the action plan.
- Take action.
- Write an action list. I keep lists in my pocket and, at times, put yellow Post-it notes on my wallet. Whatever is on your list for the day or week, aim to get it completed within a time frame.
- Get yourself a coach or a good team of people around you that have experience of what you are trying to do. The Word of God and the Holy Spirit are the best coaches that you can get. *'Without counsel, purposes are disappointed, but in the multitude of counsellors they are established.'*
- Aim to frequently catch up with yourself, report to yourself where you are – what you need to do – what needs to be done, weekly!
- Be prepared to give yourself a review of where you are in the plan of action.
- If finances are involved, make sure you track the business plan and supporting financial reporting processes within the team.
- Reward yourself and the team from time to time, when you reach certain milestones.

The key to success is to take massive determined action. As long as you are working towards being better tomorrow than you are today, you will be successful.

There are many more things you can do, but this chapter is to help you get started and believe that you can achieve your dreams.

As the company trademark slogan for Nike says: 'Just do it.'

In case you have any kind of doubts to make a good choice and investment into your life, just go to Ecclesiastes 11 which starts with *'Cast your bread upon the waters, for you will find it after many days.'*[14] Hopefully by now you will be starting to find and feel the new you with some determination to get involved in new plans and projects for the enhancement and betterment of yours and other people's lives, that you can affect spiritually and practically.

Endnotes

1. Proverbs 29:18
2. Jeremiah 29:11
3. Acts 16:6
4. Acts 16:9
5. Tom Peters and Robert H. Waterman Jr, *In Search of Excellence*, (Profile Books, 2004)
6. Proverbs 3:5
7. Matthew 13
8. All the information is found in the book of Nehemiah.
9. Nehemiah 4:10–23
10. 1 Peter 3:20
11. Psalms 37:23–24
12. Proverbs 23:7
13. Proverbs 15:22
14. Ecclesiastes 11

7
Divide the Inheritance With Me

‿

The backdrop of this chapter is taken from Luke 12:13–24, a part of scripture that talks about sharing a brother's inheritance and the rich man who wanted to build bigger barns for himself only.

'Someone in the crowd said to Him, "Teacher, tell my brother to divide the inheritance with me." Jesus said to him, "Man, who appointed Me a judge or an arbitrator between you?" Then He said to them, "Take heed and beware of covetousness. For a man's life does not consist in the abundance of his possessions." And He told a parable to them, saying, "The land of a rich man produced plentifully. He thought to himself, 'What shall I do, for I have no room to store my crops?' Then he said, 'This I will do: I will pull down my barns and build greater ones, and there I will store all my grain and my goods. And I will say to my soul, Soul, you have many goods laid up for many years. Take rest. Eat, drink, and be merry.' But God said to him, 'You fool! This night your soul will be required of you. Then whose will those things be which you have provided?' So is he who stores up treasure for himself, and is not rich toward God." Then He said to His disciples, "Therefore I say to you, do not be anxious for your life, what you will eat, nor for your body, what you will wear. Life is more than food, and the body is more than clothes. Consider the ravens: They neither sow nor reap,

they have neither storehouses nor barns. Yet God feeds them. How much more valuable are you than birds?'"

When we look at the Bible we should not take a single scripture or one verse or short passage in total isolation, without it being compared and contrasted with other scriptures, to make sure we have understood the whole of the passage, or a particular book in the Bible correctly. Our faith or our understanding of the Word of God should not be held up on one single fact. The Bible is complete in every way: what we preach, teach and believe from Scripture should be woven in the Old and New Testament.

People look at the parable of the lost sheep[1] and talk about the one sheep that went missing, and fail to congratulate the ninety-nine who were converted and stayed in their place waiting for the Shepherd to come back for them all. When we come across scriptures like Luke 12, we need to find a balance in what it is actually saying. Do not be frightened to compare and contrast scriptures to make sure you have understood all the avenues that the scripture might be unfolding.

Some people will read this scripture and interpret that we should not build and prepare for the future.

Some will say: stay in your place and do not move forward.

Some will say: we should let things accumulate to leave for others.

Some will say: God is not fair . . .

First of all, let me assure you there are no contradictions in the Bible. From my observations, an inheritance can be split into two buckets: the physical inheritance and the spiritual inheritance. A physical inheritance is something that most of us – if not all – will think about at some point in time. Even from a young age, children may have already worked out that mum and dad may be sitting on something. This is probably not a dissimilar thought to that of the prodigal son who wanted to enjoy his inheritance before his father died.

The word inheritance appears 263 times in the Bible, with additional words used meaning the same thing, such as: allotted (54 times), inherits (5), clan (96), eastward (72), assigned (64), marry (48), apportion (19); the list goes on. There may be 800-plus occurrences talking about an inheritance. This is more than references that talk about baptism, evangelism and being saved. For me, Scripture is really trying to bring out the importance of passing things down to our children, more than we may have realised. I wonder if the enemy attacks families and marriages so much to stop, delay, hold-up or make things so complicated in the inheritance process for those who are named individuals to receive.

Let me pick up one of the points above. 'Going eastward' means to move forward, to rise (like the sun rising in the morning). When Abraham remarried after Sarah had passed away, he gave all his inheritance to Isaac[2] and all his sons from his second marriage he sent eastward to Kedem. That was their inheritance, to make something of themselves in that land. Inheritance does not need to be physical money, sometimes we still need to work at what we have been blessed with to turn it into 'milk and honey'. We can get kicked when we are milking a cow or get stung by a bee when we are collecting the honey from the beehive, or we may have to climb up a rock or a tree to get to the honey and we have to overcome any fears or the dangers of falling from a great height. Or you may have to dig a well to sustain yourself and the family. These are all spiritual metaphors which we can identify with for the natural things in life too. In the beginning, in the book of Genesis, the Garden of Eden was stated as being eastward. For me, right from the beginning God has always intended to give his best to Adam and his wife Eve.

Inheritance

Inheritance was meant for the provision and status of the family. Many of the Old Testament references refer to God providing the Promised Land in the east to the Israelites.[3] This was for both the sons and the daughters. Quite simply, God introduced inheritance provision and giving for the well-being for the family in generations to come, which we cannot ignore when we are looking at scriptures relating to finances, giving, evangelism and the saving love of Jesus Christ. We cannot isolate inheritance for the people that have spiritually and practically got it together. It is for the people who think they have nothing too; they can be rich in God and have nothing practically – either one is equal.

The Bible's many laws of entitlement for those that inherit

Inheritance is very clear, with no contradictions.

God gave the Promised Land to his adopted family the Israelites. The Promised Land is his to give: 'The earth belongs to the LORD.'[4] He decides who will inherit what and when. The Israelites were not allowed to dispose of the land permanently. If, for some reason, they needed to sell the land that was given them, it would be returned to them during the year of Jubilee.[5] Even if someone had planted a vineyard or built a property on the land in the years leading up to the Jubilee, in the Jubilee year it would be returned to the original owner. The Jubilee and inheritance laws are great blessings to understand. It is good to know that God will find a way for us to get out of debt once in a while.

If you look at birth order, the firstborn son was to inherit a double portion.[6] There were no explicit instructions for inheritance if there were only females. Zelophehad[7] had five daughters and no sons by the time he died. His five daughters went to see Moses to demand that their father's inheritance must stay with them, and not be given away to his brothers or to a male from a distant relative or half relative. That would be totally unfair, as the daughters were the true next of kin. Moses then enquired of the Lord, and God said, *'The daughters of Zelophehad speak right. You will certainly give them an inheritance among their father's brothers, and you will cause the inheritance of their father to pass on to them.'*[8]

A distant kinsman could inherit the land if the father had no children.[9]

Additionally, God said that the land could not pass from one tribe to another.

The point of inheritance

Inheritance was and is a means to legally award the family and the extended family a way to support one another and survive for the future. We have choices to make to ensure we can leave an inheritance for the family, even if we fall into sickness. The Word is encouraging us to think of the future and leave something for someone, even if it is a well-used Bible or good wishes of encouragement.

When we 'pass on into eternity', we cannot take our worldly

possessions with us, but we can uphold our good wishes when we are not here to defend ourselves if we have written a will. This is not just about land and property; it is about our good wishes too. The laws provide a structure to inheritance. The laws of the land in the United Kingdom and most of the world fundamentally base their local inheritance laws on theses scriptures taken from the Bible.

Recently in the news, an individual who was omitted from their inheritance on purpose by their mother (the mother and child had a disagreement and the mother left her inheritance to a cat charity), took the case to court and the judge overturned the decision to allow the individual to receive their rightful inheritance.

In January 2016 a Lottery winner took three weeks to claim the second half of a big win. During this time there were many false claims by individuals who alleged their ticket was damaged. Many people will go to great lengths to claim something that is not theirs, even if it means contravening the law of that land.

The son of Lord Lucan was in court in February 2016 after years of chasing his inheritance. After many court hearings, he was finally able to claim what was legally his inheritance, even though his father disappeared without trace. He won the court case due to his birthright.

There is a liberty and boldness to the heirs of the inheritance of the Kingdom of God, in the physical and the spiritual. This is why when we know where we are coming from spiritually, even as the adopted child, we have a birthright from our Father in heaven.

It does not matter when things go wrong, you can still say, 'I am praising my God today because I know he has his eye on the sparrow, and I know he loves me too.'

'For through Him we both have access by one Spirit to the Father.'[10] 'We both' refers to the adopted and to the new birth person saved by his grace.

The scripture goes on to say: *'Now, therefore, you are no longer strangers and foreigners, but are fellow citizens with the saints and members of the household of God.'*[11]

Our heavenly Father provides provision as 'sons and daughters of God' or as 'adopted sons and daughters' to receive his inheritance of the Kingdom of God. This is why I love him, as he makes a way for us all to get what is ours by the new birth or adoption into his marvellous kingdom. We are not the judge who says who will or will not enter into the Kingdom of God, but we know that we will need to be one of his followers and sons and daughters. He will know us, so we should know him.

A good man

King Solomon speaks of a particular virtue in a good man relating to inheritance. It is split equally between the ability to leave something worthwhile for the future and, secondly, it is for people that you might not even have met as yet. As always this does not need to be financially focused, this can equally refer to spiritual things.

'A good man leaves an inheritance to his children's children, and the wealth of the sinner is laid up for the just.'[12]

We know that Solomon had great vision for the future. It is a sobering thought that Solomon is encouraging us to look beyond the present, to look and think into our children's children; the generations to come. God's heavenly ways are so much higher than ours on earth. Throughout this book I have been bringing to our attention and observing how God is so much different in the way that he thinks and works relating to providing and giving.

We have to play our part in preparing to provide an inheritance, so that when the inevitable happens we have prepared for the future. Even if we have been sick or out of work for decades this encouragement is still for us to have something for someone in the future. Therefore, it does not need to be financially focused; if we have not been able to save due to different issues in our lives, our positive words and prayers will not come back to us void.

However, there is an element in which we do need to have a financial inheritance to be able to give; we do have to have done something with our time on earth. It might not have been outstanding or beyond the normal, but we would have needed to come up with something that would enable us to bless others for the future.

Sometimes we just need an idea that will work for us, to till the ground, to work at something to improve us. When I started working I was earning £80 a week. I rented a room and in time was able to obtain a studio flat from the local council. At that time, I received a small government benefit to supplement my earnings and rent but, as I changed employment and earned a higher wage, I lost the benefit and had to pay the full rent which, in turn, left me with less money to live on. A slight dilemma. Yet many people face this day after day around the world.

I personally chose promotion and a change in my job role, so that I would be eligible to climb the ladder of experience in preparation for the next opportunity. Otherwise I would have stayed in a rut, and not been able to move forward. Everyone will face hard choices between quick wins for the present and immediate future, versus the choices that are slow, and sustainable choices that need to gather momentum and grow from hardship to blessings for the future.

This chapter is to encourage us to think about what we can do to enable us to put something aside each month for the future. We would need to have substance to enable us to bless generations that we might never see or meet in this world to leave a legacy.

Solomon was not just thinking of his four children Rehoboam, Menelik, Taphath and Basemath, but their children's children too. Solomon had 700 wives and 300 concubines. I am not sure how many children Solomon was really thinking about, but with this number of children he would need to have some help from God to enable the blessing to reach his children's children. For sure, Solomon's words of encouragement are still blessing every generation that reads God's Word today practically and spiritually.

Solomon was a grandparent and someday we may be blessed to become one, too, if we're not already. Grandparents are there to provide a Christian balance to the hectic life of the whole family. The grandparents are there to leave a legacy to their children's children. Solomon had his father David to live up to, as we will have ours too. Or we might not know our birth father, but we all have our heavenly Father to live up to and inspire us to go forward.

Perhaps the good man that Solomon was referring to was his father, David, or was he looking right into the future and was he was even thinking of the Messiah, Jesus Christ? Personally I think it was for all of them, especially Jesus. Looking unto Jesus the *author and finisher of our faith*.[13] As Jesus as the Good

Shepherd has thought of everything that we need to inherit from him, from faith in Jesus, to *agape* love,[14] to wisdom to the right behaviour, to the fruits of the Spirit,[15] to the gifts of the Spirit,[16] to leadership, to stewardship, from sickness to health, from darkness and being dead in sins, to becoming a new creature and being resurrected with him into his marvellous light. This is the inheritance that we need to pass down to the future generations, to make them rich in God.

To move forward, we have to do more than pray; we have to pay too. David remarked that he did not want to be in service to God if it would cost him nothing.

'*But the king said to Araunah, "No, but I will buy it from you for a price. I will not offer burnt offerings to the LORD my God that cost me nothing.*" So David bought the threshing floor and the oxen for fifty shekels of silver.'[17]

To build something funds are required. The tabernacle was built from the generosity and offering of the people. The outcome of making the decision to restore or build a new church building means we will have access to our own building.

In Luke 12, the man asking to have the inheritance shared with him and the rich man are both in the wrong; both were being governed by covetousness.[18] Scripture describes covetousness as a cloak of deceit. We do not know if the brothers are either brothers in the Lord or siblings by birth – if siblings, it may be that the younger brother was upset with the older brother's double portion. Either way, they would have been governed by Scripture. Their father's inheritance would have been shared between them fairly according to the law.

If our brother or sister by birth, or in the Lord, has more than us because their land provides more 'plentifully' than ours, or they have a double portion, we have no right to it request it, as it is theirs and not ours. Those that covet things which are not theirs break every commandment. The commandments do not just focus on love and worship towards God, they are also designed to stop people from coveting things that are not theirs – from adultery, stealing, bearing false witness, killing people, etc.

The tenth commandment provides the most detail as all the others are single sentences. '*You shall not covet your neighbour's wife, nor shall you covet your neighbour's house, his field, his male servant, his female servant, his ox, his donkey, or anything that belongs to your neighbour.*'[19]

Many of the sins today are sins of distraction, and challenges in our general lives. For example, TV programmes about other people's houses: *Grand Designs, Through the Keyhole, Escape to the Country.* It is great to get ideas of how you might carry out improvements to the home, but we need to get the balance right.

Video games like *Grand Theft Auto* and *Call of Duty* all allude to coveting things that are not ours: killing people and taking possessions. Coveting things can distract you in your spiritual life and stop you from progressing forward.

Israel could never move forward until they had set their focus on the one true living God. '*For whoever is born of God overcomes the world, and the victory that overcomes the world is our faith.*'[20]

Let me develop the balance

Our promise of inheritance is just like the Israelites'; it is from God. There are scriptures that warn us of someone trying to kill their heir to the throne, so that they would be the only one eligible to be able to pick up an inheritance that is not legally theirs to take.[21]

Inheritance comes automatically to all of us that are sanctified by his Word.[22] We obtain his inheritance by his own will.[23]

When Job was restored, he left an inheritance for his children and gave an inheritance to his daughters amongst his brethren.[24] What a great example of giving an inheritance to your children whilst you are still alive, so that you can enjoy the gift of giving and still receive guidance.

Jesus chooses to answer both men and us in a parable; this parable is for our benefit.

A parable is an earthly story with a heavenly meaning. Literally, something 'cast alongside' something else in order to illustrate that truth. Parables are a great teaching aid.

Jesus refers to the ground or the field, the land, (this is our working place, spiritual and physical).[25] The land is our field of expertise; it is where we establish ourselves. Each land may go through four seasons in twelve months. With the climate changing dramatically, it is now possible to face all four seasons in one week or even a day.

God gives us the land. In the Ten Commandments God makes a promise about the land: *'In the land which the LORD your God is giving you.'*[26] Our land needs to come from God. Our dreams need to come from God. Some people's dreams today are so often self-manufactured, or stolen from their covetous ways, as people wish to race to the top of fame. Both Daniel's and Joseph's dreams came from God. They were not relying on other people's dreams; they had dreams of their own which originated from God. What I notice today is that people see something on TV and they mimic the preacher or his structure as they do not know what spirit is sitting behind the things that they are copying.

We all have different types of land

Some vineyards are already established, and may just need upkeep. Some may be at the stage of tilling the ground, planting, watering, time of patience, harvesting, income, investing and repeating the cycle again. Some fields and lands experience famine and pestilence. Isaac experienced all of this and sowed following two famines back to back.

Isaac faced a double-dip recession and experienced 100 per cent return. Some lands will always provide a better yield than others. Each land may have issues with pests, insects, birds, diverse weather conditions and floods; yet the farmer continues all the year round, hoping, praying, believing and trusting in God that the land will provide a better yield than the year before.

The rich man is doing very well indeed and whatever he does or does not do, his land is plentiful.[27] (When you have something set up it is like a magnet: it only gets bigger.) The rich man does not consider the earth is the Lord's (remember God provides the increase). The rich man believed that his prosperity was down to him alone. The rich man has a good problem. 'What shall I do?' he said in despair. He did not pray. Proverbs lets us know to spread the increase. If the rich man took 10 per cent of his good fortune and tithed this or perhaps gave another 10 per cent to help the needy, he would have room to store his goods. Problem solved. The cycle of progression can be repeated year after year. We are the stewards of the Lord's goods to help the fatherless and the widow. *Then he said, "This I will do: I will pull down my barns and build greater ones, and there I will store all my grain and my goods.*"[28] In itself there is nothing wrong with building and progressing and going forward and increasing and being more productive.

Abraham, Job, Isaac, the daughters of Zelophehad and many more were, in their own right, always looking to progress and were very productive. They were much wealthier than we are today, but their motive to help their families and leave a Christian inheritance was their purpose, to enable them to provide a blessing to others for the future.

This rich man was only thinking about his own soul. It was the rich man's motive that was at fault. When the rich man self-praised himself, and said to his soul. *'And I will say to my soul, Soul, you have many goods laid up for many years. Take rest. Eat, drink, and be merry.*'[29] The rich man could only see himself and not see the future for anyone else.

Unlike the rich man, Joseph from Arimathea, who begged for the body of Jesus following Christ's crucifixion.[30] Joseph wrapped the body of Jesus in a clean linen cloth and laid it in his new tomb and rolled the stone over the tomb. The rich man Joseph, a disciple of Jesus, was rich in God and able to use his power and wealth to get an audience with Pilate.

The Christian who only takes care of their own soul is in the biggest danger of being the one who will be getting upset with Jesus on his return. Without physically helping someone else, our one talent is buried in our own soul. When we give to the poor, we shall not lack.

'Blessed are the meek: for they shall inherit the earth.'[31] 'Meek' in the English dictionary means humble and gentle. 'Meek' in

the Greek language means forward in spirit, predisposed, ready, willing.[32]

The people who are willing to help in the Kingdom of God will be the people that God has an inheritance for. Abraham and Job were not motivated, they were willing. For years people have tried to motivate people in conferences and training courses, spiritual and non-spiritual. In fact, motivated people that are either self-motivated or just motivated by others are in danger of working only off their motivator's emotions.

Often in the church environment, if emotions get upset, people stop attending. Going from one conference to the next, from one training course to the next, can excite individuals who may experience the highs and lows. I am not against church conferences; I have literally travelled thousands of miles to go to a church conference. Wise men travel, but they need to go beyond the emotional to find the will and purpose of God.

What I notice is that preachers who work on people's emotions miss out the main facts of the Scripture. People today are saved just by their emotions, they are like the seeds that get choked by the thorns. David Bernard wrote in his book *New Birth* that preachers should not use persuasion techniques; we need to save people by the Holy Spirit not by manipulating their emotions. People who are willing just give when they are poor or otherwise, like the widow who only had two mites and she gave all of it away. People who are willing, just do. Some people will say, 'I am not "feeling it" today so I will stay at home.' This is an emotion, not the Holy Spirit. People who are willing do not need pumping up; they can praise God even on a bad day. Remember Paul and Silas in prison.[33] People who rely on motivation will go up and down like a yoyo, or drop out of things. People who are willing keep getting better at what they do.

For seventy-eight years the British cycling team had not won any medals. They had talented people who were motivated and dedicated and practised as often as any other national team would have practised. But the British team had never even won a bronze medal. All of that changed when in 2007 Sir David Brailsford started to develop the British cycling team from the bottom up. The Sky British cycling team looked at their 'winning behaviours'.[34] The sport went from winning two gold medals in eighteen Olympic Games from 1924–2000 to accumulating eighteen in the past three Olympic Games. David's transformation project has not just affected sport; his ideas have been utilised by schools to change their exam results, as well as businesses looking to make 'marginal gains' where they can to improve in their performance. I have introduced the idea to my local church too.

Jeremy Wilson from *The Telegraph* wrote an article in May 2015 that stated: 'The basic philosophy was of a relentless and open-minded search for every conceivable improvement. So . . . British Cycling and now Team Sky have particular pillows, sleeping positions, flavoured water and hygiene strategies among their many "marginal gains".'

Each 1 per cent improvement that the team could find was presented to the team to see if they could adapt to the change and benefit from it. With all these 1 per cents adding up, they soon started to win many medals. Success is about making improvements to what you do each day, to stop repeating the bad habits, and engage with the improvements to make you better than the day before.

Team Sky turned everything upside down. Bradley Wiggins and the current team are not so much motivated, but they are willing to work unselfishly to the plan and put their bodies through the extreme for the whole team.

We need people who are willing look past the dangers and get on with it – ask the Good Samaritan. People who are willing to pray at home, in their own time, as well as at church, in their own prayer closet where nobody else can see them. *'The effective, fervent prayer of a righteous man accomplishes much.'*[35] The saints that are willing get their hands dirty, and will put their hands to the plough. The ninety-nine sheep were willing to stay in the field, while their good shepherd went looking for the lost sheep. The saints who are willing just to praise God even when the chips are down: *'yet will I praise him'*.

People who are willing do not judge people who are in need; they just know how to help them.
The rich man, though, was laying up treasures for himself, so he could eat, drink and be merry in the future, but found out it was all in vain.[36]

The Macedonian churches did not just help the Corinthian church, they also helped the poor saints in Jerusalem with a contribution without any conditions.[37] The love of God and wishing to help the poor is all part of our Christian heritage. The Spirit of a giving church, as discussed earlier in this book, just helps without any fuss, as they are just willing to help from Corinth to Jerusalem and witness to the rest of us that might look on for something to do in the Kingdom of God.

The group of churches in Macedonia were the poorest group

of churches. They had nothing in their region by which they could prosper. No rich family, everyone was equally poor. They lived hand to mouth, yet they found it in themselves to give and provide enough to be able to fund and send Titus to the richest churches in Corinth.[38] It should have been the other way around.

Consider the poorest people helping the richest. Their generosity was described as *beyond their means*. In other words, if we are willing, we move from our will to God's will, and within God's will is the power of the Holy Spirit. This is what inspired me to look into how we should be towards one another, to write this book and inspire others to help others. *'He who is in you is greater than he who is in the world.'*[39] No motivation techniques, just pure Holy Spirit. Not being covetous, yet receiving; all these things shall be added to you. The single most important thing: God wants us to find the balance, to move from coveting and, instead, be in a place where we can receive our spiritual inheritance and help others receive their spiritual inheritance too.

'But seek the kingdom of God, and all these things shall be given to you.'[40]

As I close, I ponder on the words *'beyond their means'* and wonder what this really means for us today, following the day of Pentecost as described in Acts 3. Peter and John passed one of the gates at the temple in Jerusalem called Beautiful. A lame beggar was carried there each day by his friends to receive offerings as the people passed by, as they entered the temple.

Peter looked upon this beggar and asked the beggar to look up and look on him. The beggar was thinking that he would receive some money from Peter. *'Then Peter said, "I have no silver and gold, but I give you what I have. In the name of Jesus Christ of*

Nazareth, rise up and walk."[41]

Peter held his hand, and the man's ankles and feet strengthened and the lame man leapt up and ran about totally healed, praising God for his miracle. Everyone standing around watched in amazement. After the miracle and the commotion that followed, the people looked at Peter and wondered how he did it.

Peter was very clear to the crowd and took no credit: *'Why do you marvel at this man? Or why do you stare at us, as if by our own power or piety we had made him walk?'*[42]

As Peter identified, the works of God are done in the name of Jesus; it is not because people think that we are holy or that we are special.[43] The supernatural power of God comes from God that is passed through his people that he calls to bless others.

This invisible anointing makes us look better and perform better than we can physically be responsible for. God takes us from the normal into this exceptional spiritual marginal gain that is not of our own will, but the anointing from God came upon Peter to pass on to someone in need. The means is invisible to the person involved, but the evidence is the witness of God's love and the power of the Holy Spirit.

The anointing is out of our hands. We can only start in the natural to be willing and present ourselves in the name of Jesus; to allow God to take us from the normal to allowing his power or means of the Holy Spirit to work through us to touch someone in need. That makes the impossible possible by the will of God. Miracles still happen today. We are God's vessels that allow his anointing to bless others. This invisible momentum, the surge of the Spirit comes from God. God provides the increase to whatever we are willing to put ourselves through for his service within the Kingdom of God.

By the same means, the Macedonian churches started off in their willingness to help and the momentum of the Spirit blessed the people beyond their understanding, just like when Jesus took the fives loaves of bread and the two fish to feed more than 5000 people by the Sea of Galilee.

Now it is down to us to be willing to put ourselves forward to be part of the next move of God, in the name of Jesus.

Endnotes

1. Matthew 18:12–14
2. Genesis 25:5
3. Joshua 1:1–24
4. Psalms 24:1
5. Leviticus 25:23–38
6. Deuteronomy 21:15–17
7. Numbers 27
8. Numbers 27:7
9. Numbers 27:9–11
10. Ephesians 2:18
11. Ephesians 2:19
12. Proverbs 13:22
13. Hebrews 12:2
14. *Agape* means God's unconditional love
15. Galatians 5:22–23
16. 1 Corinthians 12:8–10
17. 2 Samuel 24:24
18. 1 Thessalonians 2:5
19. Deuteronomy 5:21
20. 1 John 5:4
21. Matthew 21:38 and Mark 12:7
22. Acts 20:32
23. Ephesians 1:11
24. Job 42:15
25. Luke 12:16

26. Deuteronomy 5:16
27. Luke 12
28. Luke 12:18
29. Luke 12:19
30. Matthew 27:57–60
31. Matthew 5:5
32. Strong's Exhaustive Concordance of the Bible reference 4289 prothumos
33. Acts 16
34. http://www.teamsky.com/teamsky/staff/article/17368#3phQkYS2vBgGOyDx.97
35. James 5:16
36. Luke 12:21
37. Romans 15:26
38. 2 Corinthians 8:1–7
39. 1 John 4:4
40. Luke 12:31
41. Acts 3:6
42. Acts 3:12
43. Acts 3:16